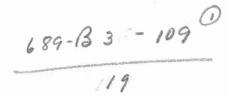

EXCHANGE-RATE DETERMINATION

CAMBRIDGE SURVEYS OF ECONOMIC LITERATURE

The literature of economics is expanding rapidly, and many subjects have changed out of recognition within the space of a few years. Perceiving the state of knowledge on fast-developing subjects is difficult for students and time-consuming for professional economists. This series of books is intended to help with this problem. Each book will be quite brief, giving a clear structure to and balanced overview of the topic, written at a level intelligible to the senior undergraduate. They will therefore be useful for teaching, but will also provide a mature yet compact presentation of the subject for economists wishing to update their knowledge outside their own specialism.

Exchange-rate determination

ANNE O. KRUEGER

Department of Economics, University of Minnesota
and *Vice-President, Economics and Research, The World Bank*

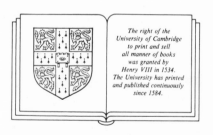

The right of the
University of Cambridge
to print and sell
all manner of books
was granted by
Henry VIII in 1534.
The University has printed
and published continuously
since 1584.

CAMBRIDGE UNIVERSITY PRESS
CAMBRIDGE
LONDON NEW YORK NEW ROCHELLE
MELBOURNE SYDNEY

Published by the Press Syndicate of the University of Cambridge
The Pitt Building, Trumpington Street, Cambridge CB2 1RP
32 East 57th Street, New York, NY 10022, USA
10 Stamford Road, Oakleigh, Melbourne 3166, Australia

First published 1983
Reprinted 1983, 1984, 1985 (twice)

Printed in the United States of America

Library of Congress Cataloging in Publication Data
Krueger, Anne O.
Exchange-rate determination
(Cambridge surveys of economic literature)
Bibliography: p.
Includes index.
1. Foreign exchange. I. Title. II. Series.
HG3851.K7   1983   332.4'56   82-14649
ISBN 0 521 25304 7 hard covers
ISBN 0 521 27301 3 paperback

CONTENTS

                                                             v

PREFACE

This volume presents a survey of the literature on the theory of exchange-rate determination. In a sense, it is a follow-up to my earlier survey of balance-of-payments theory in the *Journal of Economic Literature*. However, theory and the real world have changed so much in the intervening dozen years that this survey bears little resemblance to that earlier work.

In 1969, the field was thought of as balance-of-payments theory. Most countries pegged their exchange rates in terms of another currency (usually the American dollar) or in terms of gold. They then pursued independent monetary and fiscal policies and were confronted with policy problems when their balances of payments showed substantial net decreases in official reserves. Hence, balance-of-payments theory was addressed to the question of the determinants of the overall balance of payments and its components, with a view to analyzing the circumstances under which alternative policies (including exchange-rate changes) might alter it.

In the world of the 1950s and 1960s it was not unnatural for international economists to focus largely on the determinants of the current-account balance. One reason was that it was only as the 1960s progressed that international capital movements began to loom large in the international economy. Another was that in a fixed-exchange-rate world, speculators appeared to use changes in current-account balances as a signaling device regarding currencies that might come under pressure for exchange-rate changes.

In the early 1970s, however, the United States and Britain abandoned the fixed-exchange-rate system that had provided the underpinning for the Bretton Woods system and the enormous expansion and liberalization of international trade and capital movements in the post–World War II period. The facts that exchange rates were, at least in large part, determined by market forces after 1973 and that the movements in exchange rates, at least to some observers, appeared larger than had been anticipated led theorists to shift their attention to the determinants of the exchange rate (as an endogenous variable) and away from the determinants of the balance of payments. In addition, the increasing importance and integration of international capital markets led to a focus on the capital account as an element in exchange-rate determination.

Hence, both the title and the subject matter of the field have been altered since the late 1960s. The idea of undertaking this survey first arose in 1977. At that time, the monetary approach to the balance of payments had reached ascendancy, and a stocktaking of the field seemed appropriate. In hindsight, it is easy to see that ferment in the field of exchange-rate determination was just beginning, because the literature has mushroomed in the subsequent four years. By 1981 its exponential growth rate had shown no signs of diminishing. In part because it became clear that the field was not close to settling down, and in part because it seemed that a survey might nonetheless be useful in placing the transformation of the preceding decade in perspective, it was decided that June 1981 would be a cutoff point. No materials that were not available to me by that date, either in manuscript or printed form, have been included in this survey. Although there has been a strong temptation to bend the rule for a few critical articles, it has been resisted on the grounds that the work would be further delayed.

This survey, therefore, is designed to place current research and thinking about exchange-rate determination in perspective. It is not a definitive statement of "the" theory of exchange-rate determination, largely because there are still many unresolved questions and, in some cases, competing theories. It is intended to cover the analytical issues and underlying theory of exchange-rate determination as perceived in the early 1980s.

In the course of sifting through the literature and successive drafts of the manuscript, I have benefited greatly from helpful comments from a number of people, none of whom bears responsibility for sins of omission or viewpoints expressed. Elhanan Helpman and Assaf Razin read the penultimate draft of the entire manuscript and made many helpful comments and suggestions during a stimulating and rewarding visit to the Tel Aviv University. Max Corden was a conscientious commentator on two drafts of the material that is now Chapters 3, 4, and 5. Peter Kenen made some highly useful and constructive suggestions on the entire manuscript. Richard Snape read and commented on the first four chapters.

A research grant (SES–8106206) from the National Science Foundation permitted me to complete the manuscript in the summer of 1981. I am grateful to the foundation for its support.

I also thank Kristine O'Brien for the preparation of the indexes.

Finally, I am deeply indebted to Mrs. Delma Burns, who patiently and painstakingly typed successive versions of the manuscript, pointed out inconsistencies, and went far beyond duty in consolidating the references and rearranging footnotes.

August 1982
Minneapolis, Minn.   Anne O. Krueger

1

Introduction

To anyone interested in the question whether ideas influence events or events determine ideas, the behavior of the international monetary system and the evolution of economists' ideas about it in the period since World War II should make a fascinating case study. The questions asked by economists obviously have been influenced by the existing system and the way in which it apparently functions. Equally, economists' answers to those questions have constituted a factor that has shaped policymakers' decisions about alterations in the system. Those alterations, in turn, have changed the questions being asked.

This volume is intended to provide a survey of thought about exchange-rate determination as it emerged in the decade of the 1970s. However, this survey differs from many, because the field itself has been in a state of rapid change. An understanding of these changes and the reasons for them is therefore essential if the reader is to have a basis for understanding future advances in knowledge (and the further evolution of the system).

This chapter, therefore, will first present an overview of the evolution of the system and the analyses of it. On the basis of that, a "reader's guide" to the questions addressed and the models employed in the remainder of the volume is set forth.

1.1 **The Bretton Woods system and its aftermath**

Planning for the international economy after the end of World War II was based, naturally enough, on the hope that the perceived defects of the international economy in the inter-war period could be corrected. It will be recalled that the 1920s had witnessed three important developments: the British struggle to return to the gold standard, with a high cost in terms of unemployment and forgone real income; the difficulties experienced with reparations payments by Germany to the Allies; the emergence and then collapse of large-scale international financial flows.

That collapse, in turn, was a factor in the Great Depression. Among other phenomena that accompanied the depression, international monetary events were all highly visible and played a role of some magnitude.[1] These included competitive devaluations, erections of increasingly higher tariff walls, huge shrinkages in both the volume and value of international trade, and finally the abandonment of the gold standard. Thus, it was not unreasonable to believe that the structure of the international economy at the end of World War II should provide safeguards against repetition of these perceived evils.

To that end, one of the major international planning enterprises carried out during the war (along with that for the United Nations) pertained to structures and arrangements for handling international transactions. The structure of the postwar system, or at least the charter underlying the evolution of the system, was finally agreed on at the Bretton Woods conference, held in Bretton Woods, New Hampshire, in 1944.[2] The basic perceptions as to what had gone wrong in the 1930s – competitive devaluations, beggar-thy-neighbor trade policies, adherence to the gold standard in the face of high costs in terms of domestic

---

[1] The reader interested in further detail about the Great Depression, especially its international aspects, can consult Kindleberger (1973) and the references contained in that study.

[2] For a description of the Bretton Woods conference and its outcome, see Williamson (1977).

unemployment – motivated many of the key provisions of the plan.

All signatories to the Bretton Woods agreement joined the International Monetary Fund (IMF). Its function was to monitor exchange rates between countries so that countries could devalue their currencies when in a "situation of fundamental disequilibrium," thereby avoiding problems of high domestic unemployment and simultaneously preventing countries from undertaking competitive devaluations to improve their own positions at the expense of their neighbors. The postwar system was thus envisaged to be one of fixed, but adjustable, exchange rates.

Countries deemed not to be in fundamental disequilibrium but with balance-of-payments difficulties attributable to temporary factors were to be assisted with credits from the IMF. The intention was to prevent unnecessary devaluations and simultaneously to forestall the need for deflationary domestic policies that would have resulted in high-cost unemployment and forgone income.

Most major trading countries became signatories to the Bretton Woods documents and the IMF charter.[3] The founders were optimistic that they had ushered in a new era of "fixed, but adjustable," exchange rates that would prevent (1) the deflationary pressures resulting from correction of payments deficits under the gold standard and (2) competitive devaluations.

Despite their intentions, the international monetary system did not emerge full-blown at the end of World War II, but rather evolved as the pressure of events interacted with IMF arrangements and countries' own interests. The dollar emerged as a strong currency, and "dollar shortage" was the hallmark of the international economy in the late 1940s and early 1950s.

---

[3] It was intended that there should also be an International Trade Organization (ITO) to coordinate trade relations. However, the U.S. Senate failed to ratify the treaty. The General Agreement on Trade and Tariffs (GATT) has in practice filled many of the ITO's intended functions.

In part, this resulted in convertibility of the dollar, as contrasted with the great restrictions placed on uses of other monies. During the 1950s, however, the European countries and Japan were able gradually to relax their restrictions surrounding the uses of their currencies, and current-account transactions (i.e., purchases of goods and services) became increasingly liberalized during the decade.

Contrary to the intention that exchange rates should be adjusted as required, the Bretton Woods system as it evolved became increasingly a fixed-exchange-rate system. Countries were reluctant to devalue, and they did so only after other measures that might have ameliorated the situation had been tried and had failed. Surplus countries, by contrast, were under no pressure to appreciate their currencies, and they did so only by relatively small amounts, after great delays, when subjected to strong international pressures (including speculative flows, which will be discussed later).

These features of the system motivated the central questions addressed by economists in the late 1950s and 1960s and the assumptions they made about the conditions under which the international system operated. Because exchange rates were essentially fixed, a central question arose: What determines the balance of payments? This question led immediately to consideration of alternative policy measures that might be taken in the event of a "deficit" in the balance of payments and their probable impact on the balance of payments. Because it became evident that there were major shortcomings in the fixed-exchange-rate/periodic-large-scale-devaluation system, a second central question arose: What are the merits of fixed-exchange-rate systems relative to a flexible-exchange-rate system? Hence, the focus was on the functioning of the two alternative systems in response to a variety of shocks that might affect international transactions. Analyses of these questions will be presented in later chapters, but at this point it must be noted that the economics profession was overwhelmingly of the view that flexible exchange rates would be vastly superior to fixed exchange rates.

Finally, the third central question of the 1950s and 1960s centered on the role of the dollar as a "key currency" and as a provider of international liquidity, given that other internationally acceptable sources of liquidity – primarily gold – were growing much more slowly than was the volume of world trade.

In the world of the 1950s, capital flows between countries were relatively small compared with the value of commodity trade. They were generally closely regulated by governments even after current-account transactions had been liberalized. For this reason, the central questions of "balance-of-payments theory" were usually analyzed in the context of models that assumed little, if any, role for endogenous capital flows between countries.[4] To be sure, it was assumed that there were official capital flows, because countries could under fixed exchange rates alter their reserves in response to current-account deficits and surpluses. But the assumption that nationals of one country might alter their purchases or their holdings of assets denominated in foreign currencies was not incorporated into models designed to address any of the three questions. Thus, as of the late 1960s, that branch of international economics dealing with the international monetary system and arrangements between countries for financing exchanges of goods and services focused largely on determinants of the balance of payments (including the way in which devaluation might affect it) in the context of models in which only current-account transactions were endogenous. Hence, the name balance-of-payments theory could readily be given to the subject matter, which focused on the interrelationships between monetary variables such as relative prices and trade flows.

Much of the analysis that emerged during the 1950s and

---

[4] An exception to this general statement was the two-instruments/two-targets approach of Mundell, Fleming, and others discussed in Section 4.3.1. In the Mundell-Fleming model, capital flows were assumed responsive to interest-rate differentials. That insight later proved to be the starting point for the "monetary approach to the balance of payments."

1960s remains valid today, at least under the assumptions of the models then employed. That analysis will be surveyed in Chapter 3. For present purposes, the point is somewhat different: The main body of that analysis pinpointed some fundamental difficulties with the fixed-exchange-rate/periodic-devaluation system, as well as difficulties with reliance on the dollar as the major source of increases in international liquidity. It was widely recognized that continued support of an exchange rate, by drawing down reserves to satisfy the private sector's excess demand for foreign exchange, could only invite speculative activities as individuals anticipated currency devaluations. As that happened, Central Banks would be forced to abandon their efforts to support the par value of their currency more and more rapidly.

It was also recognized that the system of international liquidity, theoretically based on gold as the main form of international reserves, but in fact increasingly based on dollar holdings, also constituted a source of potential difficulty for the system: In order for international liquidity to increase, the United States had to incur payments deficits (as conventionally measured) in order to supply international reserves. That, in turn, provided an important source of asymmetry in the system that constituted a focal point for analysis.[5]

Any reading of the history of the international economy in the 1970s must lead to a verdict that the core of the analysis emerging from balance-of-payments theory was fundamentally correct: The system was unsustainable. The period of the late 1960s and early 1970s simultaneously witnessed two phenomena: (1) continued integration of the world economy as capital flows became increasingly sensitive to interest-rate differentials

---

[5] Another type of asymmetry, also analyzed in the literature, but not central to the argument here, concerned the fact that deficit countries were generally under more pressure to devalue than surplus countries were to appreciate, thereby imparting an inflationary bias to the system (and ensuring that the demand for international liquidity would increase).

and the world capital market became increasingly integrated and (2) abandonment of the fixed-exchange-rate system, at least as it functioned in earlier years, by the major trading nations.

The increased mobility of international financial capital has fundamentally altered the environment within which international economic variables operate and thus has changed the nature of the models relevant for analysis of international monetary phenomena. Simultaneously, the abandonment of the system of exchange rates fixed within very narrow bounds has provided a host of empirical evidence about the behavior of exchange rates when determined, at least partially, by market forces. The empirical evidence suggests that exchange rates have fluctuated rather more than had been anticipated by the proponents of the flexible rate system. Simultaneously, it no longer makes sense to ask what determines changes in central-government international reserves on the assumption that the price of foreign exchange is rigidly fixed. Because the behavior of exchange rates has puzzled observers, and because exchange rates are more endogenously determined than they were in the 1950s and 1960s, the focus of analysis has shifted in large part to asking what determines the behavior of the exchange rate and, for that matter, what the function of the exchange rate is.

As if a changed institutional structure and consequently altered questions were not enough, the shifting focus in the past decade has been complicated by the fact that macroeconomic theory itself has been in a state of flux. Many of the balance-of-payments models of the 1950s and 1960s assumed relatively simple Keynesian structures of a domestic economy, with the price of domestic output given. Aggregate demand therefore played a key role in influencing the level of economic activity.

In the 1970s, by contrast, there has been widespread recognition of the possible roles of rigid real or nominal wages and other types of market imperfections that might serve as a backdrop for macroeconomic behavior. Simultaneously, increasing attention has been given to individuals' expectations of public policy as a factor influencing their actions. It has come to be recognized that policy actions that are fully anticipated by the public will have no impact at the time they are taken: Individual decision makers will have taken full account of them in making their plans.

There is probably no area of analysis in which the role of expectations is potentially more important than in the behavior of exchange rates. The models of exchange-rate determination have therefore not only incorporated the changed institutional structure but also taken into account economists' improved understanding of the role of expectations, especially about economic policy, and the way those expectations influence observations of policy responses.

For all these reasons, international monetary economics has changed markedly in the past decade. The focus of analysis has shifted. The validity of some of the underlying assumptions of earlier models has been questioned, and new assumptions have been made. The underlying macroeconomic structure of trading economies has also been reexamined.

Moreover, the transition is not yet complete. Just as macroeconomic theory is being confronted by empirical evidence that only uncomfortably fits received doctrine and is therefore subject to challenge, so too the unfolding of the world's experience with flexible exchange rates (which are, after all, phenomena of the past decade) will provide new challenges and necessitate continuing amendments to the basic model and the questions underlying international monetary economics.

1.2 Outline of the volume

This survey is intended to reach nonspecialist professional economists whose balance-of-payments theory was learned prior to the 1970s, as well as to provide graduate students and advanced undergraduates with an up-to-date account of the field. A major problem in any survey is delimiting the subject matter to be covered, and in this case the problem was perhaps even more severe than usual. An initial decision, taken out of necessity, given the volume of material, was that the survey would cover contributions to analysis but would not extend to empirical testing or results. A second decision was to focus only on exchange-rate determination and the effects of changes in exchange rates.

In most respects, the theory of exchange-rate determination is based on an analytical structure equivalent to that used to analyze the determinants of the balance of payments under fixed exchange rates. The difference, of course, is that the shifts in excess demand for foreign exchange lead to quantity adjustments under fixed rates and price adjustments under flexible rates. Thus, attention turns first to exchange-rate, or balance-of-payments, determination. Thereafter, formal analyses of differences and similarities between the functioning of the alternative systems are considered.

Whereas this leaves a very broad subject area for coverage, it implies a nationalistic focus of the volume, and it omits questions such as international monetary integration,[6] optimal levels of international reserves and liquidity, and the entire range of questions that surround consideration of an optimal international monetary order. Nonetheless, it reflects the focus of the profession and the mainstream of research in the 1970s.

Finally, new material has been forthcoming at a very rapid rate, but in the interest of completing this volume it was decided that no information would be included that became available after June of 1981. In some instances, working papers were available at that time that have since appeared in print, and the citations for those items have been changed. Otherwise, works that became available to the author after June 1981 have been left unread, for fear that the temptation for further alterations would prove irresistible.

The organization of the survey is as follows. Chapter 2 covers preliminary material, including key definitions and concepts

---

[6] For an exposition of the underlying issues of economic integration, see Allen and Kenen (1980, Parts IV and V).

used throughout the volume, and the range of questions falling within the domain of what will be called "exchange-rate-economics," as a shorthand. Chapter 3 then presents models of exchange-rate determination and the balance of payments centering on the current account. These include the more traditional models of the 1950s and 1960s referred to earlier. Chapter 4 then covers models of exchange-rate determination when the capital account is the sole mover of the exchange rate. Chapter 5 focuses on models of interaction between capital account and current account in exchange-rate determination. Chapter 6 is then addressed to the effects of alternative exchange-rate determination mechanisms on domestic macroeconomic variables. It is assumed that an increase in aggregate demand increases output, at least somewhat. The mechanisms are fixed and flexible exchange rates and limited intervention under various rules. Chapter 7 provides an introduction to models of exchange-rate/macroeconomic interaction under alternative macroeconomic assumptions, including rigidity of the real wage, fix-price models of disequilibrium, and sectoral models. Chapter 8, finally, covers the effects of exchange-rate changes under exchange-control regimes, when the capital account is suppressed, and where current-account transactions are subject to restriction.

2

The field, the questions, and the concepts

The first task of this chapter is to define the scope of exchange-rate theory. As already mentioned, exchange-rate theory encompasses the theory of exchange-rate determination under flexible rates, analysis of the determinants of the balance of payments under fixed rates, and the role of the exchange rate under exchange control. The first section contains a guide to the nature of the questions addressed and motivation for the study of the field. A second section introduces some basic concepts: the current account, the capital account, purchasing-power parity, and so on. A final section then attempts a taxonomy of models in terms of the questions asked and the assumptions made about institutional surroundings and individual behavior.

2.1 Exchange-rate theory

International economics has always been that branch of applied economics dealing with economic relationships among nations. As such, it has relied heavily on basic economic theory – both macro and micro – for its tools of analysis, drawing on both branches as has seemed best to fit the problem at hand.

A first question, therefore, is why the existence of sovereign states alters economic analysis. After all, normal models of an economy might be the entire world. For some purposes, the answer is that internationality may not change things. For example, any economic analysis of the grain market must be an analysis of the world market. Yet, by and large, the fact that the market is international does not make the analysis essentially different from the analysis that would be used for the Australian fruit and vegetable market, for example.

For other purposes, there may be meaningful distinctions between models applicable to "an economy" and models applicable to some sorts of international economic relations. One such class of models has focused on the higher degree of mobility (or differential productivity in different uses) of factors of production within countries than between them. These models, both Ricardian and Heckscher-Ohlin-Samuelson (HOS), provide the basis for analyzing the effects of international trade between countries among whom factors or production are not mobile.[1]

A second class of models focuses on policies that countries adopt discriminating between goods based on their origin or destination. Thus, there is a large body of theory of "commercial policy," which provides a basis for analyzing the effects of tariffs, quotas, export subsidies, "dumping," taxes on earnings of foreign investors, and so on. These policies are all typically not adopted within countries (although taxes may have effects rather similar to tariffs) but are resorted to between them. Closely related to this literature is a body of analysis of the effects of various domestic policies on international competitive position (e.g., value-added taxes in Europe and corporate income taxes in America).

Generally speaking, both of these types of analysis focus on "real" variables in the economic system: relative prices of goods and factors of production, quantities of goods exported and

---

[1] To the extent that factors of production are not mobile between regions, the "international" models may be more applicable to interregional trade than are models of perfect factor mobility. Conversely, factors may be highly mobile between some pairs of countries, and that may alter the appropriate framework for analysis of transactions between them.

imported, and so on. A third type of analysis focuses on those aspects of international economic relations that pertain to, or are influenced by, payments arrangements for international transactions. Here, the essential feature is that most countries have their own national currencies, and there are alternative ways in which they can permit their monies to be used for international transactions. A question underlying the entire field is the degree to which the exchange rate is a real variable. The answer may depend on the mechanisms chosen for carrying out international payments.

An examination of those mechanisms and their effects under various institutional arrangements constitutes the core of exchange-rate theory. On one hand, countries may legislate that their currencies are to be "inconvertible," that is, not freely exchangeable for other currencies, and may strictly license international transactions.[2] In such circumstances, the licensing mechanisms used have significant effects on relative prices in the domestic economy, but little effect on monetary aggregates. At the other extreme, a country may choose to fix its exchange rate in perpetuity with respect to some international money.[3] If all transactions were freely permitted, the country would essentially have chosen to abandon its "monetary sovereignty," as its money supply would be determined via a price-specie-flow mechanism (see Section 2.2.5 for a definition).

Most countries' arrangements for international payments have been somewhere between these two extremes. There are two dimensions. Some countries have permitted relatively free convertibility for current-account transactions, but have imposed restrictions on capital-account transactions, whereas others have imposed virtually no restrictions on international financial transactions of any kind. Likewise, some countries

---

[2] This is the International Monetary Fund definition of convertibility, and the one used throughout this volume.

[3] A sovereign country could always reverse any such commitment. It could therefore be argued that the extreme no-independent-money case can never exist between nations.

have fixed a par value for the exchange rate, but have occasionally altered it in response to pressures. Other countries have permitted the exchange rate to be determined in the foreign-exchange market, but have intervened to a greater or lesser extent, giving rise to the phenomenon termed the "managed float."

The questions arising for economic analysis are several: (1) What are the positive and normative effects of current-account convertibility with capital-account inconvertibility? (2) What are the mechanisms by which a country can adjust to a shift in its current-account balance, and what are the implications of the alternatives? (3) How do the conclusions reached alter with capital-account convertibility when domestic and foreign assets are substitutable?[4] (4) Can countries have independent monetary and fiscal policies, and to what extent do their international-payment arrangements lead to a loss of control over the money supply?

As even this brief discussion indicates, exchange-rate theory draws on all branches of the core discipline to analyze phenomena arising out of countries' arrangements for settling their international transactions. By 1980, a large part of that theory centered on exchange-rate determination, although in fact the theory of exchange-rate determination under flexible exchange rates is in most respects the counterpart to balance-of-payments theory under fixed exchange rates. Emphasis has shifted from asking how quantities change under fixed exchange rates to how prices change under flexible rates, but the two questions are very closely related.

When countries maintain fairly fully convertible currencies, exchange-rate theory is almost like a branch of monetary economics (except that devaluation or the flexible-exchange-rate alternative is not available within a unified currency area). At

---

[4] If there were no substitutability between domestic and foreign assets, capital would be immobile, and capital-account inconvertibility would be redundant.

the other extreme, when currencies are inconvertible and all transactions are subject to license, analysis of the effects of exchange-rate changes comes very close to the analysis of tariffs and quotas, and money moves well away from center stage. As the international-payment system has evolved since the Bretton Woods agreement, currency convertibility has increased greatly; consequently, exchange-rate theory relies somewhat more on monetary theory and has moved further away from the theory of commercial policy than was earlier the case.

While that shift in emphasis has taken place, one fundamental insight has remained unchanged, an insight that is central to exchange-rate theory: The purpose of international-payment arrangements is to facilitate the smooth functioning of international transactions in goods, services, and assets. Therefore, alternative payment mechanisms and government policies pertaining to them can be evaluated in terms of how well they carry out that function. An international-payment arrangement is not an end in itself, but a means by which other objectives can be achieved.

Finally, exchange-rate theory focuses on analysis of the effects of various exchange-rate arrangements on variables of interest. It is distinguished from international finance in that the latter is concerned to a greater extent with the specific institutional arrangements of particular means of payment (letters of credit, Eurodollars, etc.) and "how to do it." Exchange-rate theory, by contrast, abstracts from the particular details of payment and, instead, examines the ways in which particular classes of arrangements (fixed exchange rates, flexible exchange rates, etc.) affect the economic system in general and the international economy in particular.

2.2 Basic concepts of international-payment theory

In this section, some ideas and concepts used repeatedly throughout the field of exchange-rate theory are introduced. In some cases (such as purchasing-power parity) the concepts are also testable hypotheses and are not always empirically valid.

In other cases it is a simple matter of setting terminology straight.

2.2.1 *Exchange-rate concepts*

The exchange rate is the price at which one national money can be exchanged for another (when transactions are permitted). To speak of the exchange rate increasing or decreasing is terminologically ambiguous. It is preferable to speak of changes in the price of foreign exchange. Generally, if one mentions "exchange-rate depreciation," what is meant is that the price of foreign exchange in the country in question is becoming dearer; that is, a unit of domestic currency is worth relatively less than was previously the case. Obviously, an increase in the price of foreign exchange from the viewpoint of the home country is a decrease in the price of that country's currency for the rest of the world.[5]

Cross-rates. There are as many spot exchange rates for a country as it has trading partners with independent currencies. Thus, there is a dollar–franc rate, a dollar–pound rate, a dollar–mark rate, and so on. In practice, it usually is sufficient to speak in terms of a single exchange rate, because cross-rates of exchange are always closely aligned through arbitrage.[6] Thus, if one knows the franc–dollar exchange rate and the mark–dollar

---

[5] The terminological difficulty with "exchange rate" is mirrored in financial practices for exchange-rate quotations: These can be given either as the number of local currency units per unit of foreign exchange or as the number of units of foreign exchange a local currency unit will purchase. Historically, Britain followed the latter procedure, whereas the United States (and many other countries) followed the former. For some purposes (such as measuring the percentage change associated with a discrete devaluation) it is important to specify which measure is being used.

[6] When opportunities for profitable transactions arise because of a misalignment of rates (such as might occur between the Midwest and the New York stock exchanges, for example), the act of buying where cheaper and selling where dearer is referred to as arbitrage. When arbitrage is sufficiently close to being perfect, rates are linked together by a margin equal to transactions costs (including the arbitragers' time). The foreign-exchange market is one in which arbitrage generally appears to be fairly perfect.

exchange rate, one can easily infer the franc–mark rate, at least within very narrow limits. This is because the cost of exchanging currencies is generally miniscule. There will be foreign-exchange traders ready to buy and sell currencies if the cross-rates diverge by any appreciable margin.

Countries generally intervene in their foreign-exchange markets, if at all, with only one currency or only a few currencies (the "intervention" currency). If a country buys its own currency (selling the intervention currency), this will tend to appreciate it in terms of the intervention currency, and the country can safely assume that the prices of all other currencies will decline in proportion with the intervention currency.

Nominal and effective exchange rates. Until the advent of floating rates in the 1970s, most countries registered "par values" for their currencies with the IMF in line with the Bretton Woods rules. Such a par value was the official exchange rate. In many instances, however, countries would, in their reluctance to devalue, impose "transactions taxes" or surcharges on purchases of foreign exchange. For that reason, it became useful to distinguish between nominal exchange rates (i.e., the rate registered with the IMF and quoted as the official rate) and effective exchange rates, which reflected the prices actually paid and received by traders for foreign exchange. To be sure, once exchange surcharges were imposed, there were often different effective exchange rates for different classes of transactions.

In recent years, under flexible rates, a second meaning of the term "effective exchange rate" has become widespread: It has been applied to a weighted average of trading partners' exchange rates with the country in question. Thus, a country facing appreciation of the mark and yen and depreciation of the dollar and pound might calculate a trade-weighted average of those exchange rates to determine its effective rate.

Some major trading countries are now allowing their exchange rates to fluctuate and to be at least partially market-determined. However, a number of smaller trading nations continue to peg their currencies to that of one of the larger countries or to a "basket" of currencies. Because surcharges can still be imposed in those cases, the effective-exchange-rate concept remains useful to distinguish between the stated rate and the rate relevant for decision makers.

Purchasing-power-parity/price-level-adjusted (PPP/PLA) exchange rate.[7] Especially when a country is experiencing rapid inflation, it is useful to distinguish nominal and effective exchange rates from their "real" counterparts. The notion is that the relevant concept for the real exchange rate is the nominal rate adjusted for differentials in inflation rates[8] between the home country and the partner country.[9] Thus, the PPP/PLA exchange rate is the exchange rate divided by the home country's price index and multiplied by the partner country's price index.

Forward and spot rates. The spot exchange rate is the rate prevailing for purchases or sales effected at the time the rate is quoted. The forward exchange rate is the exchange rate at which a contract can be signed at that same time to buy or sell foreign exchange in the future (forward). Under certain conditions, to be discussed later, the forward and spot exchange rates may be linked through interest arbitrage (whereby the difference between the two rates is equal to the interest-rate differential plus or minus transactions costs).

2.2.2 *Components of the balance of payments*

The balance of payments is a record of all international transactions. Like all double-entry-bookkeeping accounts, it

---

[7] Note that this is a definition of an exchange-rate concept, not the purchasing-power-parity theorem to be discussed later.

[8] There is a sizable literature accumulating as to what the relevant price index should be. That issue will be discussed in later chapters.

[9] Note that, at this point, cross-rates may diverge significantly. In such cases, "the" PPP/PLA exchange rate or effective exchange rate would have to be a weighted average of PPP/PLA rates. For further discussion, see Chapter 8.

always balances. Whenever an exporter consigns goods to a foreign destination, there is always a credit instrument or other payment flowing in the opposite direction (unless it is a gift). Because both sides are recorded, the sum of all credit entries equals the sum of all debits.

What is important, therefore, is a breakdown of balance-of-payments items into categories that permit meaningful analysis. Which breakdown, if any, is most meaningful may well depend on the question being asked, as well as the nature of the payments regime under which transactions are being recorded. In this discussion we shall identify some of the distinctions that prove useful in a wide variety of models of international payments.

Current account. The current account is a double-entry-book-keeping record of all flows of goods and services between countries. Thus, as its name implies, it is the sum of current transactions. Exports, imports, tourist expenditures, dividend and interest income flowing to and received from abroad, insurance and shipping payments and receipts, and other flow transactions are recorded in it.[10] The current-account balance is the difference between credits (exports, income from tourists, dividend and interest income from abroad, etc.) and debits (imports, tourist expenditures abroad, etc.).

Capital account. The capital account is a record of all asset transactions between a country and the rest of the world. Borrowing from abroad, purchases of securities from abroad, and drawing down a foreign bank account are all capital-account

---

[10] Private remittances (usually from immigrants or guest workers) usually are recorded in the current account. Government transfers (foreign aid) often are recorded as a separate item, in neither the current account nor the capital account, but insofar as they are a flow transaction, repeated period after period, it probably makes sense conceptually to regard them as entering into the current account. For purposes of reconciliation with national-income accounts, all transfers are current-account items.

transactions. Sometimes a distinction is made between short-term and long-term capital transactions, although for present purposes that distinction need not detain us. Obviously, when taken together, the net capital-account position (credits minus debits) is equal to, and opposite in sign from, the net current account. The net capital account also records the extent to which the country's net indebtedness to foreigners has altered during the period covered by the balance-of-payments statistics.

The distinction within the capital account that is of some importance is between those transactions undertaken in the normal course of affairs and those transactions undertaken by the government either as a residual under fixed exchange rates or intended to affect the exchange rate (under flexible exchange rates). In practice, it is impossible to tell whether government actions were undertaken for normal purposes or for balance-of-payments reasons, but usually an effort is made to identify the deficit in the balance of payments (under fixed rates) with the amount of government intervention. Thus, at a fixed exchange rate, if the government intervenes in the market to affect the exchange rate, the government is regarded as being in surplus if it is buying more foreign exchange than it sells (i.e., it is accumulating foreign assets or paying off liabilities to foreigners), whereas it is in deficit if it is selling foreign assets (or borrowing abroad).

Empirically, there are several measures of deficit or surplus, each of which attempts to measure some relevant concept of the net government position.[11] From the viewpoint of theory, however, one can assume that the means of financing the deficit (or the assets accumulated via the surplus) are clearly identifiable, and alternative empirical measures of the deficit or surplus need

---

[11] In the fixed-exchange-rate period, some writers distinguished between "autonomous" and "induced" capital flows. The latter were defined to be those associated with government support of the exchange rate. Once it was recognized that the government could affect the exchange rate by means of monetary policy (thus influencing private capital flows), it became clear that the distinction was arbitrary and was not empirically useful.

not be of concern. Conceptually, the deficit or surplus is simply the change in the government's net foreign-asset position (including its indebtedness) arising from its activities in financing international transactions.

2.2.3 *Exchange-rate systems*

Although there are varying degrees of currency convertibility, it is useful to distinguish three separate types of exchange systems and to apply the distinction separately to current-account and capital-account transactions. They are fixed exchange rates, flexible exchange rates, and exchange control.

A fixed-exchange-rate system is a convertible-currency system in which individuals are free to undertake their desired transactions at prevailing prices and in which the government buys and sells foreign exchange in order to maintain the exchange rate.[12] Under this system, the major questions are the following: (1) What circumstances can lead to deficits or surpluses in payments, and are they likely to be transitory or sustained? (2) What alternative courses of action are open to a government when it is faced with persistent deficits or surpluses? It may also be useful to inquire as to the meaning of capital-account inconvertibility if residents are free to undertake their desired current-account transactions at prevailing prices.[13]

A flexible-exchange-rate system is a convertible-currency system in which the exchange rate is market-determined and in which there can be no deficit. (In practice, governments intervene under flexible exchange rates, but the focus here is on pro-

---

[12] It should be noted that a fixed-exchange-rate system is compatible with the presence of tariffs and other charges on international transactions.

[13] In recent years, a number of countries have adopted a "sliding-peg" exchange-rate system, under which the exchange rate is fixed, although it is altered by small amounts at frequent intervals to adjust for the differential between the country's inflation rate and that for the rest of the world. Depite these adjustments, the system is a fixed-rate system for purposes of analysis (see Section 8.3).

totypes for analysis, as in Section 6.3.) The central question pertains to the determinants of the exchange rate and changes in the exchange rate.

Finally, an exchange-control system is one in which the government sets the exchange rate and does not necessarily let individuals carry out their desired transactions. Foreign exchange is sold only under certain conditions, and individuals generally are required to sell any foreign exchange they may have to the government. In such a system the currency is inconvertible. Although there are numerous mechanisms used for allocating foreign exchange under exchange control, a simple mechanism that is useful as a prototype is to imagine the government each day counting the amount of foreign exchange sold to it and then selling the foreign exchange the next day (perhaps at the official exchange rate) to certain selected groups of buyers, leaving other willing buyers unable to purchase foreign exchange in their desired quantities.

2.2.4 *Openness of the economy*

A useful concept throughout analysis of alternative exchange-rate systems is that of an open economy. An open economy is defined as one in which domestic disturbances (such as increased demand for imports or reduced supply of exports) spill over into the international marketplace as excess quantities of goods and services demanded or supplied. International disturbances (such as altered terms of trade) are directly reflected in domestic variables, and especially in domestic prices. In a closed economy, domestic disturbances are fully reflected in domestic supply and demand and price adjustments, and the comparative statics of disturbances can be analyzed without regard to external behavior.[14]

An economy may be closed for purposes of some types of analysis and open for others. For example, if there is exchange control on current-account transactions, shifts in the demand

---

[14] See the discussion in Section 8.1.

for importable goods will be reflected in changes in domestic prices. However, fluctuations in the world prices of major exportables may be fully reflected in domestic markets. An interesting application of the concept of openness relates to the insulation of the domestic economy (in the macro sense) from international disturbances and the ability of the domestic monetary authority to control the money supply.

2.2.5 *Price-specie-flow mechanism*

Suppose that a particular country were to fix its exchange rate with respect to, say, the American dollar and then were to issue domestic money only to the extent that it held American dollars in its Central Bank. Then, if there were a deficit in its balance of payments, the monetary authority would be paying out dollars, and the domestic money supply would be shrinking.

As that happened, individuals' desired levels of expenditures on foreign goods would decline,[15] and simultaneously domestic goods would appear more attractive to foreigners. Consequently, the deficit (i.e., the amount by which dollar holdings were declining) would diminish. This process would continue until the deficit was eliminated.

Conversely, if there were a surplus in the balance of payments, the Central Bank's holdings of dollars would increase, and so it would increase the domestic money supply. Expenditures on foreign goods and services would increase while the supply of exportables available to foreigners would be reduced. Consequently, export earnings would tend to shrink while expenditures on imports rose, thus making the surplus smaller. This mechanism is known as the price-specie-flow mechanism. It will be seen in Chapter 3 that it is the underlying prototype

---

[15] The reasons for this decline may vary with the particular model specified. It might be that domestic prices of home goods are declining relative to tradables. Alternatively, there might be a real balance effect as individuals attempt to restore their liquidity.

of one sort of adjustment mechanism under fixed exchange rates.

2.2.6 *Purchasing-power-parity theorem*

The purchasing-power-parity (PPP) theorem essentially asserts that prices in one country must equal those in another country when expressed in a common currency. Depending on the model at hand, the PPP theorem can be stated as an arbitrage condition (i.e., in the absence of transport costs, prices of traded goods must be equal everywhere simply through arbitrage) or as a proposition pertaining only to tradable goods. There are two versions: In one, it is absolute prices that are equalized, whereas in the other, it is only proportionate rates of price-level change that are reflected in proportional movements in exchange rates.[16] PPP can hold because exchange rates determine prices, or conversely. PPP can be assumed to hold through arbitrage, or it can be a theory of exchange-rate or price-level determination (see Section 4.1.1).

2.3 **Types of models**

There are large numbers of payments regimes and even greater numbers of domestic economic structures against which the operation of these regimes can be modeled. As a consequence, there is a bewildering variety of models of various aspects of international payments. It is hoped that the initial outline of types of models presented in this section will prove useful as a frame of reference for the more detailed analyses of later chapters.

Essentially, models can be characterized in seven ways, on the basis of various factors: (1) the questions they ask; (2) the assumed nature of the international environment; (3) the assumed macroeconomic structure of the domestic economy;

---

[16] Here, as earlier, there are important questions as to which price index should be used for measurement. That topic will be covered in Section 4.1.1.

(4) the treatment of capital-account transactions, both bonds and money; (5) the assumed links between current-account transactions and the domestic economy; (6) the extent to which the model is what we shall call "closed" over time; and (7) the assumptions about expectations formation and their role. Some of these categorizations require more comment than others. But, as will be seen, there are several possibilities under most of these headings, and hence the number of possible models is exceptionally large.

2.3.1 *Questions*

Chief among the questions asked are these: (1) What are the properties of fixed- and flexible-exchange-rate systems (a) in handling domestic and foreign shocks and (b) in affecting the economy's response to domestic policy measures? (2) What are the alternative means of adjustment to external and/or internal disturbances under fixed exchange rates, and what are the determinants of the exchange rates under flexible rates? (3) What are the properties of alternative systems (taking into account the variety of possible regimes to be discussed later and including exchange control) in their facilitation of international transactions?

Clearly, answers to any of these questions will hinge on the assumptions made with respect to each of the items to be discussed later. There are also logical links between the questions. For example, an analysis of how an economy will respond to easier monetary policy under fixed and flexible exchange rates will also provide insight into alternative means of adjustment and determinants of exchange rates.

2.3.2 *The international environment*

There is a large class of models dealing with a "small" economy, by which is meant that some of the external parameters confronting it cannot be affected by the country's action. Thus, the world price of tradable goods may be assumed fixed, or the world interest rate may be assumed given, with an infinitely elastic world demand and supply of credit to the country in question.

There is a second group of models dealing with only one economy, but some of the external parameters of these models may be functions of the country's own behavior on world markets. Thus, the terms of trade may be a function of the quantity of excess supply of exportables and importables, or the borrowing rate from abroad may be a function of the quantity borrowed.

Finally, some models are of a general-equilibrium nature, because they are solved for equilibrium values of variables in "both" countries (where one country can generally be interpreted as "the rest of the world").

2.3.3 *The domestic economy*

Obviously, the variables of interest in the domestic economy can be many and varied. First, there is the obvious difference between neoclassical models and all others. In the neoclassical models, all domestic markets are assumed to function perfectly, so that full employment is always maintained. Nonneoclassical models can vary in a number of regards. They can be of a relatively simple Keynesian structure, in which the price of domestic output or level of the money wage rate is given and the level of output is determined by aggregate demand. Alternatively, some simple Phillips-curve mechanism can be built into the economy's specification so that output can increase only with an increase in the price level. Still other specifications include fix-price disequilibrium models and models that treat sectoral issues. Finally, in recent years there has come to be an important distinction between economies in which nominal wages are sticky downward and economies in which wages are largely indexed, so that it is the real wage that is rigid downward.

2.3.4 *Capital-account treatment*

It is in connection with the capital account that much recent work has been done, and attention is given in Chapter 4 to various detailed specifications of the capital account. For present purposes, we need only note that some models assume only current-account transactions, some assume that domestic residents can hold foreign bonds but foreign residents cannot hold domestic bonds, some assume that bonds but not foreign money can be held, and so on.

2.3.5 *Links between current account and the domestic economy*

Here, the most crucial issues are whether traded goods produced domestically are perfect or imperfect substitutes for traded goods obtainable from the rest of the world and whether or not there is a class of nontraded, or home, goods.[17] If all goods are traded, and if domestically produced goods are perfect substitutes for foreign goods, the scope for any payments mechanism to affect the domestic economy is very limited. This is because all excess-demand schedules are so highly elastic that it is difficult to find a meaningful role for an exchange-rate or macroeconomic variable.

2.3.6 *Treatment over time*

As already noted, there can be a payments imbalance only to the extent that a country's net indebtedness vis-à-vis the rest of the world changes. For this reason, treatment of the issue of changing asset positions over time is of crucial importance for analysis, especially if one is contrasting alternative payments mechanisms. Some models break into the process at an unspecified midpoint and do not come to grips explicitly with changing asset positions. Such was the case, for example, in analyses of the effects of devaluation in the 1950s and 1960s.

---

[17] In international-trade theory, the important criterion is whether or not a good is tradable. Tradables that are not traded presumably either are priced between the f.o.b. and the c.i.f. international price or are subject to prohibitive protection. For exchange-rate theory, the price of a good that is not traded behaves like that for a home good, and the important distinction is between traded and nontraded goods.

2.3.7 *Expectations formation and their role*

As with other components in the macroeconomic literature, treatment of expectations varies widely across different classes of models. In some analyses of devaluation it is assumed that the devaluation is unanticipated but that the newly fixed exchange rate is expected to remain at its existing level in perpetuity. At the other extreme are models of payment mechanisms in which international transactions are dominated by the capital account and in which expectations about the future path of the interest rate must be rational and must play a large part in determining the time paths of the exchange rate, the interest rate, and the price level.

2.4 **Summary**

As this enumeration indicates, the possible combinations of assumptions are very many. As is usually the case in economic analysis, it is useful to start by attempting to understand what would happen in a neoclassical environment in which all participants were rational maximizing agents. Much recent work on the theory of exchange-rate determination has been an effort to do just that. Before getting to those topics in Chapters 4 to 6, it is necessary first to examine older, more traditional models in Chapter 3.

3

Models of the current account

Any meaningful model that is to be useful in analyzing one or more aspects of exchange-rate determination must somehow grapple with the fundamental proposition that if consumers optimize subject to their budget constraints, then there can be excess demand in one market only if there is excess supply in another. Moreover, if there are n markets, with the demand relations for each being derived from optimizing behavior, then there will be only $n - 1$ independent (excess) demand relations.

Thus, if there are only two goods in the model, excess demand for one will be identically equal to excess supply of the other. In that case, analysis of the market for one good is all that is necessary for full analysis; the supply and demand relations for the other will not be independent. To be sure, assumptions about behavior in the market under examination have implications for the omitted market.

These considerations immediately highlight two essential features of exchange-rate theory: (1) The apparently trivial exercise of designating one market as the dependent one and dropping it from analysis can lead to entirely different foci of analysis for different analysts. (2) In terms of a two-good model, one cannot begin to analyze the effect of an exchange-rate change on excess demand unless the excess rate is itself the relative price of the two goods in question. In a two-good model there can be no analysis of anything even loosely identifiable with a "payments deficit," because all exchanges (in or out of equilibrium) have two sides. One could regard one good as commodities and the other as assets and permit trade between countries. One country would then be able to consume more now relative to later, while the other country would do the converse, acquiring assets from the spending country. As is evident from that description, such a model focuses on the capital account, and therefore it will be considered in Chapter 4.

In this chapter we seek to analyze simple models in which there is trade in commodities, but in which a deficit is in principle possible. Such a model must contain at least tradable goods (which may or may not be a composite commodity) and another asset that individuals may hold. In an important sense, then, this chapter is designed to survey models of exchange-rate and current-account determination in conjunction with a payments mechanism. Much of the discussion is couched in terms of the effect of an exchange-rate change (devaluation) on other variables of interest, because the literature originated in the fixed-exchange-rate world of the 1950s and 1960s. However, the analysis is quite symmetric, so that one can think of (ex ante) shifts in the other variables having their impact on the exchange rate.

For expository purposes, it is useful to start by reviewing the elasticities–absorption controversy of the 1950s and 1960s. That debate highlighted many of the issues in the theory of exchange-rate determination and motivated the current-account models set forth later in this chapter. The elasticities and absorption approaches, and the debate over them, are covered in Section 3.1. In Section 3.2, a simple model with money and a composite tradable good is developed. It is then used to analyze the properties of a price-specie-flow mechanism, a fixed exchange rate, and a flexible-exchange-rate payments system. Then the model is amended to incorporate the existence of home goods and their impact on relative prices.

The reader should bear in mind two considerations throughout this chapter. First, exchange-control mechanisms are not considered here; an analysis of their effects will be presented in Chapter 8. Second, the analysis set forth here abstracts from issues associated with the capital account. Interesting questions that concern the links between the current account and the capital account and their interaction in affecting the exchange rate or the payments deficit will not be considered until Chapter 5.

3.1 The elasticities–absorption controversy

If one were to ask what the most widely known model of balance of payments or exchange-rate determination is, the answer would surely be the elasticities approach. That approach is so widely known and used that its validity and limitations must be well understood. In this section, therefore, the condition will first be presented. Next, the Keynesian multiplier models will be briefly set forth. Then the absorption approach (which built on the Keynesian insights) and its criticisms of the elasticities model will be covered. Next, we shall consider Dornbusch's derivation of the conditions under which the elasticities formula might be valid. Then we shall introduce the J-curve possibility that the short-run response of the current account to an exchange-rate change may be perverse.

3.1.1 *The simple elasticities approach*

In its simplest possible form, the elasticities approach is based on some variant of the following overly simplified model. Define p as the relative price of the importable in terms of the exportable. Then

$$M = M(p) \tag{3.1}$$
$$X = X(p) \tag{3.2}$$
$$B = X - p_m M \tag{3.3}$$

Equation (3.1) sets forth a demand-for-imports function. Equation (3.2) gives the export function ($X' > 0$). Equation (3.3) gives the balance of payments. It is implicitly assumed that devaluation changes p. To ascertain the effects of a devaluation, substitute (3.1) and (3.2) into (3.3) and differentiate totally:

$$dB = \frac{\partial X}{\partial p_x} dp_x - p_m \frac{\partial M}{\partial p_m} dp_m - M \, dp_m \qquad (3.4)$$

Defining $\eta_x = (\partial X/\partial p_x)(p_x/X)$ and $\eta_m = -(\partial M/\partial p_m)(p_m/M)$, letting $p = p_m/p_x$, and dividing by p yields

$$\frac{dB}{dp} = \frac{X}{p}(\eta_x + \eta_m - 1) \qquad (3.5)$$

In its alternative formulations [see equation (3.12) for the Bickerdicke-Robinson-Metzler formula], elasticities can be decomposed into export supply and demand elasticities and import supply and demand elasticities separately for each of two countries. For present purposes, equation (3.5) is sufficient. For, in any of the elasticity-approach formulations, a change in the exchange rate is identified with a change in some relative (and hence real) price within the system. Once this is done, it seems straightforward by inspection of (3.5) that elasticities might have the "right" sign, and yet devaluation (i.e., the change in p) might fail to improve the trade balance of the current account.

In its many variants, it was the elasticities formula that gave intellectual support to the notion of elasticities pessimism: It was apparently not enough for demand curves to be downward-sloping and supply curves upward-sloping. Evidently, sufficiently low elasticities might lead to failure of the current-account balance to improve consequent to devaluation.[1] The intuitive interpretation given to this result was that whereas devaluation would necessarily increase export earnings, it might

---

[1] In many of these models it was assumed that the capital-account "autonomous" balance was unaffected by exchange-rate changes. Note that if devaluation had failed to improve the relevant balance, appreciation would have. See Kemp (1970) and Krueger (1974).

not reduce total foreign-exchange expenditures on imports if demand were price-inelastic. A smaller volume of imports might nonetheless be accompanied by larger demand for foreign exchange.[2] To see why modern theory rejects this simple approach, it is necessary to consider Keynesian views and their criticisms of this approach.

3.1.2 *Keynesian aggregate-demand models*

It was only natural, following the Keynesian revolution, that multiplier-based analyses of the effects of exchange-rate changes would be developed. Most of these were based on one variant or another of the following relation:

$$B = B(Y, R/P) \tag{3.6}$$

where B is the trade (or current-account) balance, Y is the level of real output, R is the price of foreign exchange, and P is the domestic price level. The change in reserves is the sum of B and the capital-flows component of the balance of payments separately determined.

The partial derivative of B with respect to Y is assumed to be negative. This is generally rationalized as being because exports are exogenously determined (by foreign-demand levels, presumably), whereas imports are a function of the level of real income and expenditures.

Thus, the current account unequivocally deteriorates with increases in the level of real income: Not only do imports of goods and services rise while exports are unaffected, but any associated increase in the domestic price level resulting from the

---

[2] In interpreting the elasticities condition, it is useful to have in mind a stability theorem from trade theory. In a two-commodity barter model, it is necessary for stability that, starting at equilibrium with zero excess supply, an increase in the price of one commodity results in excess supply of that commodity. Formally, the requirement is that $n - n^* + m - m^* < 0$, where n and n^* are home and foreign compensated price elasticities of excess demand and m and m^* are home and foreign marginal propensities to spend on the commodity. See Jones (1961) for a full treatment.

increase in real income further tends to "worsen" the current-account balance.[3]

This simple aggregate-demand approach was employed in several ways. Meade (1951) used it to illustrate countries' possible situations under a regime of fixed exchange rates. If countries were in current-account deficit (and wished to reduce the size of the deficit) while simultaneously they were experiencing inflationary pressures, the objectives of internal balance (full employment) and external balance would be compatible: Reductions in aggregate demand would reduce inflationary pressures and tend to increase the size of the current-account deficit.[4] Countries with underemployment and current-account surpluses likewise were deemed to have compatible objectives. However, if improvement in the current account and increases in real output were policy objectives, then internal-balance and external-balance objectives were in conflict; likewise if reducing a current-account surplus and reducing the rate of inflation were objectives.[5]

Obviously, the internal-balance/external-balance analysis rests on very partial specification of the underlying macroeconomic model. For present purposes, however, there is another point. If a conflict between external balance and internal balance were deemed to exist, the case for altering the exchange rate as an instrument to achieve external balance would be strong. For, in aggregate-demand models, the exchange rate was seen as an instrument that could free the domestic economy from constraints imposed by the balance of payments. Domestic

---

[3] These models often then assume that capital flows are sensitive to interest-rate differentials, so that increases in real income can be accompanied by no loss of reserves if the interest rate is permitted to rise (see Chapter 4).

[4] Note that this formulation perceives "inflationary pressure" to be a once-and-for-all change in the price level.

[5] There is a disequilibrium interpretation of the Meade model. If domestic prices are fixed in the short run, then real income can be altered only by changing the current account or the exchange rate. See Chapter 7 for a discussion of disequilibrium models.

monetary and fiscal policy can be geared to achieve domestic objectives. This conflict was the "fundamental disequilibrium" anticipated in the Bretton Woods document.

It was this line of reasoning that underlay the expenditure-switching, expenditure-reducing analysis of the policy imperatives imposed by a payments deficit, as pioneered by Johnson (1958). There the essential notion was that at less than full employment, external balance could properly be maintained by expenditure-switching policies, presumably exchange-rate adjustments. In circumstances of a current-account deficit and underemployment, Johnson (following Meade) argued that correction of the deficit could come about primarily through inducing consumers to demand more nontraded goods and fewer traded goods. For this, the exchange rate was the optimal instrument, rather than exchange controls.

Under full employment and inflation, however, it was recognized that one could not switch expenditures away from traded goods without also resorting to an expenditure-reducing policy; otherwise, an increase in the price level would be the only outcome. Hence, at full employment, correction of a current-account payments deficit would require both expenditure switching (to release resources for export and reduce the demand for imports) and expenditure reduction, in order that resources would be available.[6]

3.1.3 *The absorption approach*

Although Meade clearly saw the expenditure implications of unbalanced current-account positions, it was Alexander (1952) who put the case in a way that highlighted the difficulty with the elasticities approach. His starting point was "the identity, that the foreign balance, B, is equal to the difference between the total production of goods and services, Y, and the

---

[6] See Chapter 7 for some modern disequilibrium models and sticky-real-wage models of the relationship between the current account and the exchange rate in post-Keynesian terms.

total absorption of goods and services, *A*" (Caves and Johnson, 1968, p. 361).

Alexander's central question was how devaluation might change the relationship between expenditures, or absorption, and income, in both nominal and real terms (because the identity holds both ways). As he put it, there are "three basic questions: how does the devaluation affect income? How does a change in the level of income affect absorption . . .? How does the devaluation directly affect absorption at any given level of income?" (Caves and Johnson, 1968, p. 362). Clearly, the elasticities approach sheds little light on these questions.

Indeed, the formulation of Alexander's questions highlights the inadequacies of the elasticities approach. And yet, given that the exchange rate is the price of foreign currency in terms of domestic currency, an entirely income-oriented analysis of the effects of exchange-rate changes also seemed unsatisfactory. This apparent conflict between price-based analysis and income-based analysis of exchange-rate determination and the balance of payments was the central focal point of analysis in the 1960s.

With the benefit of the work of the 1960s and 1970s, most of the elements of the puzzle have been resolved. They focus on the exchange rate as playing a role in determination of the relative prices of tradable goods and home goods, as affecting real balances, and as affecting intertemporal allocation of expenditures relative to income. Those concerns will be dealt with later. Here, the central question is whether or not we can find a satisfactory modern interpretation of the elasticities approach.

3.1.4 *Modern interpretation of the elasticities approach*

The reader will probably conclude that the elasticities approach is a poor tool for analysis – either analytical or empirical. Nonetheless, as Dornbusch has pointed out, "these shortcomings notwithstanding, the model continues to enjoy substantial popularity in policy discussions and interpretations of current events, in empirical work, and in recent textbooks . . .

The . . . model is likely to remain the preferred tool in the analysis of trade balance issues" (Dornbusch, 1975*b*, p. 859).

Suppose, following Dornbusch (1975*b*), we form the following model:

$$M(P_m) = X^*(P_m^*) \tag{3.7}$$

$$X(P_x) = M^*(P_x^*) \tag{3.8}$$

$$B = P_x X - P_m M \tag{3.9}$$

$$P_m = P_m^* R \tag{3.10}$$

$$P_x = P_x^* R \tag{3.11}$$

where asterisks denote variables in the foreign country, M and X are imports and exports, P's are prices, and R is the home country's price of a unit of foreign exchange.

Defining ϵ and ϵ^* as the home and foreign elasticities of supply of exports and n and n^* as the absolute values of the compensated price elasticities of demand for imports, the "elasticities condition" can be derived as

$$\frac{dB}{dR} = \frac{P_x X}{R} \frac{nn^*(1 + \epsilon + \epsilon^*) - \epsilon\epsilon^*(1 - n - n^*)}{(\epsilon + n^*)(\epsilon + n)}$$

$$(3.12)$$

This is the Bickerdicke-Robinson-Metzler (BRM) or Marshall-Lerner condition for trade-balance improvement consequent to devaluation.

It is, at first sight, a disturbing formula for a variety of reasons: (1) The formula appears to relate to absolute, rather than relative, prices. (2) Without some third commodity in the background, there can be no difference between expenditures and income; otherwise, the budget constraint would appear to be violated. (3) Even if (3.12) is satisfied, it is not evident how devaluation lowers expenditure relative to income.

Early efforts to grapple with the BRM condition focused largely on the partial-equilibrium nature of the model and on derivation of alternative stability conditions (including primarily gross substitutability), as in the work of Hahn (1959) and Negishi.

More recently, Dornbusch (1975*b*) and Jones (1974) have explored the conditions under which the formula can be valid.[7] Essentially, the conditions are quite stringent. One must specify what market is omitted from the equation system (3.7) through (3.11). The most plausible omitted market is that for home goods; to render (3.12) valid, the marginal propensity to spend on home goods would have to be unity and that on traded goods zero. This rules out the general-equilibrium effects that made earlier authors believe that the condition was essentially one of partial equilibrium. In addition, however, there must be a specification of the devaluing country's monetary and fiscal policy that, in the background, induces the adjustment of expenditure relative to income that is required for devaluation to improve the current account.[8] Dornbusch showed that one such mechanism would be a home-country monetary and fiscal policy geared toward maintaining a constant nominal price of home goods.[9] Taxes would thus be increased whenever the exchange rate was devalued. This would remove the excess demand for home goods that would otherwise arise as consumers attempted to substitute home goods for traded goods.

Thus, in this interpretation, a devaluation raises the nominal (and therefore relative) price of tradables. Consumers tend to switch expenditures toward home goods, thus driving up the nominal price of home goods. The monetary and fiscal authorities thereupon are obliged to levy an income tax to reduce demand for home goods sufficiently to prevent their price from rising. Such increased tax receipts constitute the source of

---

[7] Kemp's Appendix (1962), which appears not to have been widely noticed, contains an analysis very similar to Dornbusch's treatment.

[8] As Dornbusch showed, it clearly makes a difference what is being held constant by the monetary and fiscal authority: It might be the nominal supply of money, nominal wages, or nominal income. Holding the nominal price of home goods constant is but one alternative.

[9] There must also be zero cross-price effects between traded goods, a condition that Negishi (1968) had earlier derived.

expenditure reduction accompanying devaluation (and the net increases in taxes equal the improvements in the trade balance).

Finally, the possibility of (3.12) failing to be positive can arise, even granting the strongly restrictive assumptions, only when the terms of trade deteriorate. With home goods understood to be the third commodity, there is no presumption whatever that they would deteriorate. If the terms of trade improve or are unchanged for the devaluing country, there is no way in which dB/dE can be negative.

Thus, the elasticities condition is now seen as a very special case in which monetary and fiscal policy is assumed to be operating in a particular way in the background, while all income effects pertain only to home goods. Insofar as one normally associates the need for exchange-rate changes with domestic macroeconomic imbalances, this assumption may be regarded as being close to assuming away the problem under investigation. Even then the BRM condition can fail to be satisfied only in the event of a deterioration in the terms of trade, which would be a side outcome of the transfer entailed in the devaluation itself.

3.1.5 *The J curve*

Although the elasticities condition is no longer interpreted to imply that devaluation might "fail," there is an alternative basis on which questions have been raised about the short-term effects of exchange-rate changes on the current account. Although it is based more on empirical observations than on theory, it has important theoretical implications. That is, it is quite possible that flows of goods and services respond only with time lags to changes in the exchange rate.

This proposition, termed the J curve, emanates from the observation that at the time an exchange-rate change occurs, goods already in transit and under contract have been purchased, and the completion of those transactions dominates the short-term change in the current-account balance. The J-curve term is used to describe the movement over time of the current-account balance: It may deteriorate at first as exports denominated in domestic currency in shipping contracts earn less foreign exchange, while imports may be paid for in foreign exchange. The initial impact of a depreciation of the exchange rate could therefore be that foreign-exchange expenditures would be unaltered while foreign-exchange receipts would be declining. Magee (1973) characterized the phenomenon as consisting of a period during which contracts already in force in specified currencies dominate the determinants of the current account (the currency contract period). Over time, new contracts, made after the exchange-rate depreciation, begin to dominate, and the "pass-through" of the devaluation, or depreciation, is effected.

Obviously, the extent to which there is a J curve depends on the extent to which trade takes place under preexisting contracts (as contrasted with purchases in the spot market), the degree to which there may be asymmetric use of domestic currency and foreign currency in making contracts,[10] and the length of the lags in the execution of contracts. There might be countries for which there is no negatively sloped behavior of the current account over time in response to exchange-rate changes, whereas others might have particularly prolonged periods of perverse response. Although the possibility rests largely on the empirical considerations associated with time lags and the currency denomination of contracts, it assumes importance for the modeling of exchange-rate determination because the existence of the J curve would imply that, in the short-run, the foreign-exchange market might be unstable in the absence of capital mobility. It thus pinpoints the crucial nature of assumptions about the capital account for analyses of exchange-rate determination and effects of exchange-rate changes, a subject to which we shall return in the next chapter.

---

[10] For empirical evidence that there may be asymmetries, see Grassman (1973). Recently, Razin (1981) has rigorously shown that there are differences in monetary responses depending on whether contracts are denominated in buyer's currency or seller's currency.

3.2 **Money and tradable goods**

One early effort to reconcile the expenditure-absorption and relative-price aspects of exchange-rate changes was through the introduction of an asset, money, into the model. Kemp (1962), Dornbusch (1973*b*), and Michaely (1960) all focused on the real-balance effect of an exchange-rate change.

It is simplest to start by assuming a small country, faced with given international prices for all the commodities it produces and consumes. The small-country assumption permits treatment of all commodities as a single composite good, because their relative prices are fixed. Full employment and competitive pricing of goods and services are assumed to prevail in the home market. Thus, the country's real income and the vector of real outputs are determined.

Obviously, if consumers derived their incomes from the production of traded commodities, and if they maximized utility subject to a budget constraint where their incomes equaled their expenditures, the country's balance of payments would be identically zero (everywhere, not simply at equilibrium). The exchange rate would be redundant in the analysis in the sense that all exchange rates would yield the same relative prices, the same real incomes, and the same expenditure patterns.[11]

To introduce a payment mechanism into the system, therefore, it is necessary to introduce a role for money. One way or another, all neoclassical models of the payment mechanism for current account posit expenditure functions of a form such that expenditures increase or decrease relative to income as desired cash balances fall short of or exceed actual money holdings.[12]

---

[11] Note, however, that the exchange rate would determine the price level. Presumably, then, the money supply would be an endogenous variable (see Section 4.1).

[12] This can be justified by using the Cambridge equation (Dornbusch, 1973*a*), assuming the demand for money is proportional to expenditures (Kemp, 1962), or assuming that money enters the utility function, which is separable in consumption and real balances. Michaely (1960) was among the first to use the real-balance effect as a major component of balance-of-payments responses to exchange-rate changes.

Thus, excess-demand functions, E_i, are assumed to take the form

$$E_i = E_i(P_1, \ldots, P_i, \ldots, P_n; M^* - M) \qquad (3.13)$$

where P's are the prices of the n commodities (in domestic currency), M^* is desired nominal balances, and M is the stock of money. The partial derivatives of the E_i functions with respect to $M^* - M$ are assumed to be negative.

Introducing an exchange rate (price of foreign currency), R, domestic prices are equal to foreign prices, Q's, times the exchange rate:

$$P_i = RQ_i \quad (i = 1, \ldots, n) \qquad (3.14)$$

Now define the balance of payments, B, measured in foreign currency, as

$$B \equiv - \sum_{i=1}^{n} Q_i E_i \qquad (3.15)$$

Assume that for a given money stock, $\overline{M}$, and an initial exchange rate, $\overline{R}$, B equals zero. This, of course, implies that desired nominal balances equal the actual money stock, $\overline{M}$. Assume further that world prices, the Q_i's, are unaffected by a small country's actions. To investigate the effect of an exchange-rate change, (3.15) can be differentiated to yield

$$\frac{dB}{dR} = - \sum_{i=1}^{n} \left(\frac{\partial E_i}{\partial P_i} \frac{\partial P_i}{\partial R} + \cdots + \frac{\partial E_i}{\partial P_j} \frac{\partial P_j}{\partial R} \right.$$

$$\left. + \cdots + \frac{\partial E_i}{\partial (M^* - M)} \frac{\partial (M^* - M)}{\partial R} \right) Q_i \quad (i \neq j) \quad (3.16)$$

Because initially $M^* = M$, the homogeneity property implies that at the initial equilibrium,

$$\sum_{j=1}^{n} \frac{\partial E_i}{\partial P_j} P_j = 0$$

Because $\partial P_i / \partial R = 1$, because foreign prices are given, and $Q_i = P_i / R$, equation (3.16) becomes

$$\frac{dB}{dR} = -\sum_{i=1}^{n} Q_i \frac{\partial E_i}{\partial (M^* - M)} \frac{\partial (M^* - M)}{\partial R} \quad (3.17)$$

Because the demand for nominal money holdings increases with the price level, which increases with the exchange rate, the right-hand term of (3.17) is positive, and the left-hand term is negative, by assumption that excess demand for commodities is a decreasing function of the gap between desired and actual money holdings. B therefore unequivocally increases with an increased price of foreign exchange (i.e., devaluation or depreciation). The trade balance, B, which is the same as the balance of payments, "improves" by the amount that individuals hoard to restore their initial real cash balances. The trade balance is equal to the excess demand for money.

Several comments are in order. First, if the nominal money stock $\overline{M}$ is held constant (the surplus sterilized), the balance of payments, B, will continue to be positive. That is, B is a flow. If, instead, the surplus is monetized, consumer expenditures will increase, and the surplus will go to zero. Had the initial assumption been that individuals reduce their expenditures by a fraction of the amount by which they wish to increase their desired holdings, it would not affect the qualitative results, because all signs would remain unchanged. The first-period surplus would simply be a fraction of the difference between desired balances and money holdings. Nor would partial adjustment affect the result that the size of B would be unaltered period after period if the surpluses or deficit were sterilized.

If, however, the balance-of-payments surplus is not sterilized, but instead augments the country's money stock, the size of the surplus will diminish over time until it finally reattains zero. This, of course, is the price-specie-flow mechanism. Under that mechanism, a devaluation results in an increase in the domestic price level, which then induces individuals to reduce their real expenditures to restore their initial real cash balances. Once those balances are restored, the values of all real variables in the system return to their initial levels, and the long-run effects of the exchange rate are only on the price level and nominal balances.

Second, as set up, equations (3.13) through (3.16) treat the exchange rate as exogenous. One could, instead, let the exchange rate be endogenously determined so as to keep B equal to zero and then investigate its response to say, a once-and-for-all increase in the money stock, an upward shift in the demand for real balances, or a transfer from abroad. With a once-and-for-all increase in the money stock there would be one-shot depreciation of the currency, proportionately equal to the increase in the money stock. Real variables in the system would be unaffected.[13]

Third, the model highlights a fundamental property of all balance-of-payments models: An excess demand for goods can exist only if there is an excess supply of something else, presumably money. This leads immediately to the distinction between momentary equilibrium (in which all individuals are carrying out their desired flow transactions given their initial stocks) and stock-flow equilibrium (in which stocks and flows are both at desired long-run levels). It also focuses on the difficulty that is involved with attempting to discuss a "deficit" on current account: That deficit must be accompanied by a surplus on capital account, and the Walrasian dependence between the two implies that it makes as much sense to focus on the money market as it does to focus on the goods market in analyzing the payment mechanism. Worse yet, focusing on the former implies analysis of behavior of stocks, whereas focusing on the latter emphasizes flows. It will be seen in later chapters that a promising means of coming to grips with this problem lies in examining stock-flow linkages.

[13] One could also examine the effect of an expected sustained constant rate of increase in the money stock. It makes little sense to do so, however, until interest rates are introduced into the model, a subject deferred until Chapter 4.

Fourth, the model is only a partial-equilibrium representation of a payment mechanism. First, the payment imbalances incurred by the home country are presumably offset by changes in the holdings by the rest of the world of the country's money stock or of some other asset. An important question is why, in the case of sterilizing a deficit or surplus, the rest of the world should be willing to accumulate the country's money in exchange for goods. In addition, even if we posit that the price-specie-flow mechanism works in the rest of the world as well, so that levels of money-stock holdings change, there is no guarantee that the rest of the world's hoarding function will be the same (but opposite in sign) as the domestic hoarding function.

It is relatively straightforward to amend the model so that world equilibrium holds (Kemp, 1962, 1970; Dornbusch, 1973*b*). All that needs to be done is to add the requirement that hoarding in the home country equal dishoarding in the rest of the world. Then, in response to a devaluation by the home country, the home country's price level rises, and that in the other country (rest of the world) falls in proportion such that the amount by which domestic residents wish to increase their real balances equals the amount by which foreigners wish to reduce theirs, given the initial change induced by the price-level changes. The act of augmenting or running down cash balances can impact on the other real variables of the system only when there is a relative price to be affected.[14] This could happen in the monetary model presented here if the marginal propensities to spend on some commodities differed between countries.

3.3 Nontraded, or home, goods

In early Keynesian models of balance-of-payments adjustment, each country was assumed to specialize in the production of a commodity or group of commodities, and the price of each country's produced goods was assumed given in terms

---

[14] Altering real cash balances always affects the time path of real expenditures relative to real income.

of domestic currency. Thus, an exchange-rate change was deemed automatically to be a relative price change between exports and imports, and analysis of the effects of exchange-rate changes proceeded in terms of their effects on exports, imports, and other variables. Exchange-rate changes were treated as being synonymous with terms-of-trade changes. For reasons discussed in Section 3.1, this procedure is unsatisfactory on several counts. The development of the approach in Section 3.2 solved that problem, but the model implies that all relative prices are independent of the exchange rate. To international economists, the notion that an exchange-rate change would not affect any relative price seemed somewhat unrealistic.

One way out, a way employed by Pearce (1961), Krueger (1974), and Dornbusch (1973a), is to posit the existence of a class of domestically produced and consumed nontraded goods, for which domestic markets must clear at any exchange rate.[15] Nontraded, or home, goods exist (1) because of transport costs sufficiently high that the relevant range within which the domestic price must fluctuate to clear the home market is large enough that imports or exports are never profitable or (2) because of prohibitive protection to a class of importables.[16] In

---

[15] A second, widely employed assumption is that the country under consideration is a price-taker, for its imports, but that the world price of the export is a function of how much it sells. See Dornbusch and Fischer (1980) for a recent example. This assumption implies monopoly power in trade. An alternative procedure widely employed in empirical analyses of trade problems is to assume that domestically produced tradable goods are less than perfect substitutes for foreign tradable goods. This model was first proposed by Armington (1969). Despite its great appeal in empirical work, it has not been used formally to model the role of the exchange rate. One could regard the terms-of-trade effect (discussed later) as pertaining to imperfect substitutes.

[16] For purposes of analyzing the effects of exchange-rate changes, it makes little difference whether a class of nontraded goods exists because of high transport costs or because of government prohibitions on importation (or exportation) of those goods (or even because of a sufficient amount of water in the tariff). For analyzing the welfare effects of alternative payment regimes, however, the distinction between nontradable goods and nontraded goods is crucial (see Chapter 8).

these models, a change in the exchange rate alters the price of traded goods relative to home goods. Conversely, exchange-rate changes happen because of changes in excess demand for tradables relative to home goods.

Demand functions continue to have as an argument the divergence between actual and desired money stocks, but now the prices of home goods (P_H) are endogenous to the model, and their prices, relative to the prices of traded goods, P_T, can alter. The essential features can be seen in a model with a composite home good, a composite traded good (the small-country assumption), and money:[17]

$$E_T = E_T\left(\frac{P_T}{P_H}; \frac{M^* - M}{P_H}\right); \quad \frac{\partial E_t}{\partial(P_T/P_H)} < 0,$$

$$\frac{\partial E_T}{\partial(M^* - M)} < 0 \quad (3.18)$$

$$E_H = E_H\left(\frac{P_T}{P_H}; \frac{M^* - M}{P_H}\right); \quad \frac{\partial E_H}{\partial(P_T/P_H)} > 0,$$

$$\frac{\partial E_H}{\partial(M^* - M)} < 0 \quad (3.19)$$

$$M^* = M^*(P_T, P_H, Y); \quad \frac{\partial M^*}{\partial P_T} > 0,$$

$$\frac{\partial M^*}{\partial P_H} > 0, \quad \frac{\partial M^*}{\partial Y} > 0 \quad (3.20)$$

---

[17] There are several ways in which one can evoke the constant-relative-price assumption among home goods. If the vector of world prices of tradables is given, it could then be argued that those prices are sufficient to determine the prices of factors of production, which in turn fix the price of home goods. The difficulty with this line of reasoning is that the relative price of home goods might also be fixed relative to all tradables, given the fixity of factor prices. Another line of reasoning might have all home goods, for example, labor-intensive relative to all tradables. In such a case, relative prices of tradables might not change, but a country's pattern of specialization might change in such a way that the relative price of home goods would be altered, with movements of resources between the traded and the home-goods industries.

$$B \equiv M^* - M \equiv -P_T E_T \qquad (3.21)$$
$$E_H = 0 \qquad (3.22)$$
$$P_T = RQ_T \qquad (3.23)$$

Given the parameters M (the money supply), Y (real output, given by assumptions of full employment), R (the exchange rate), and Q_T (the foreign price of tradables), the system of six equations has six variables: E_T, P_T, P_H, M^*, E_H, and B.

The first two equations give the excess demand for traded goods and home goods as a function of relative prices and the gap between actual and desired cash balances. As can be seen from the signs of the partial derivatives, an increase in desired cash holdings reduces excess demand for both home goods and traded goods. The third equation gives the demand for nominal cash balances as a function of prices of home and tradable goods and of real income. The fourth equation can be in one of two forms: Either the trade balance is equal to the difference between desired and actual money balances (or, in the more general case, the fraction of the gap that individuals wish to close in the current period) or, equivalently, the trade balance is equal to the domestic value of the excess demand for tradable goods. The two relations are not independent: The excess supply of money is equal to the excess demand for goods, as was seen earlier, and only one formulation of the trade-balance constraint is independent (the other can be derived from the budget constraint).

The new element in the home-goods model is that the excess demand for home goods must be zero at equilibrium. It is this feature that drives the model, as contrasted with the money/traded-goods model of Section 3.2. It is most readily understood in the context of a fixed-exchange-rate, variable-deficit model. Consider an initial full equilibrium in which desired and actual money balances are equal and the excess demand for traded goods is zero. Suppose that the monetary authority instantaneously increases the money supply, holding the exchange rate,

R, constant.[18] Clearly, excess demands for traded goods and for home goods will be positive at initial prices. For traded goods, the excess demand can be satisfied as long as the monetary authority sells foreign exchange for domestic currency at the given exchange rate. However, domestic production of home goods must increase. Under normal assumptions, this increase can occur only with an increase in the price of home goods (to attract resources from the traded-goods industries). Consumers will, naturally, substitute traded goods for home goods in consumption at the new, higher price of home goods.

The new equilibrium will be one in which the price of home goods has risen and in which there is a realized excess demand for traded goods (a balance-of-payments "deficit"), financed, presumably, by the monetary authority running down its supply of foreign-exchange reserves. Because that is a continuous process, the new equilibrium will be reached only after a period of time. Individuals' nominal cash balances will be larger at the new equilibrium, because the higher price of home goods will induce greater nominal cash holdings. Hence, the payments deficit will not equal the initial increase in the supply of money, because some portion of it will be absorbed by voluntary increases in money holdings.

The initial and new equilibria can be illustrated with the help of Figure 3.1, usually referred to as the Salter diagram.[19] The axes measure quantities of home goods and traded goods, and the curved line *tt* represents the transformation possibilities between *H* and *T*. A point such as *E* represents the full equilibrium: At prices represented by the slope of the tangent to the

---

[18] It is assumed that the change is unanticipated.

[19] Salter's famous 1959 article used this representation of balance-of-payments difficulties in a "dependent economy." It was one of several important articles to emerge from Australian discussions of their payments difficulties in the 1950s. Other important articles in the Australian discussion were by Corden (1960), Meade (1956), and Swan (1960). See Oppenheimer (1974) for a review of the literature on the role of home goods.

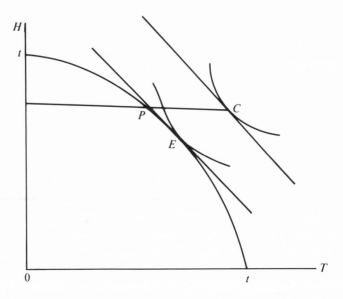

Figure 3.1. The Salter diagram.

transformation curve at E, consumer demand for home goods equals the quantity of home goods supplied, and the value of production of traded goods equals the value of consumption of traded goods. Hence, there is payments balance. After the increase in the money supply, the new equilibrium of consumption might be at a point such as C, with the production point at P, with production of home goods equal to consumption of home goods. In order for home-goods consumption to have increased, consumers must have been spending beyond their incomes as can be seen by noting that at the former budget constraint (associated with E) and a higher price of home goods, consumers would have reduced their consumption of home goods. Obviously, at C the value of domestic consumption exceeds the value of domestic production, and there is a current-account deficit equal in value to PC.

As this representation clearly shows, a payments deficit can exist only with both a higher relative price of home goods than would prevail at full equilibrium and an excess of expenditure over income. To turn the statement around, in order for a current-account deficit to be reduced through devaluation, the relative price of home goods must decline, and expenditures must fall relative to income. Both of these effects could result, with a constant money supply, from devaluation: Expenditure levels would fall as individuals attempted to restore their real cash balances (given that devaluation results in an increase in the price level via the increased price of tradables), and consequently the excess demand for both home and traded goods would decline. With a downward shift in the demand for home goods, their relative price would fall, thereby encouraging some substitution in consumption away from tradables and toward home goods.[20]

Insofar as one wants to identify a relative price effect of an exchange-rate change, it would appear that it must come through the home-goods/traded-goods price relationship. Indeed, in the models to be described in later chapters, the home-goods/traded-goods price relationship is used in a variety of different contexts more and more frequently; the "real" exchange rate is being defined as the price of tradables relative to the price of home goods.

For present purposes, three additional points need to be mentioned. First, there is the observation made by Oppenheimer (1974) that nontraded goods play their role in an analysis of devaluation only if they are not highly substitutable for traded goods both in consumption and in production. That is, if the marginal rate of transformation of home goods and traded goods in production is fairly constant over a wide range of possible outputs, there will be little relative price change, and other factors must bear the burden of adjustment: The relative prices

---

[20] In nominal terms, of course, the price of home goods would increase. But it would rise by less than the amount of devaluation, thus leading to a lower relative price.

of home goods and tradables will be fairly constant. Likewise, for the relative price of home goods to play a significant role in the adjustment process, the size of the home-goods sector must be fairly substantial: A small home-goods sector is likely to be one in which the price of home goods is determined by the price of tradables.

Second, as Berglas and Razin (1973) pointed out, there may be only one real exchange rate, defined as the relative price of traded goods to nontraded goods, at which production of traded goods will be nonspecialized. That is, if several tradable goods are produced, in the conventional HOS model that suffices to fix factor prices. With factor prices given and constant returns to scale in the production of nontradables, their price is determined under the usual competitive conditions. Changing the real exchange rate would, in that circumstance, imply moving to a specialized pattern of production in tradables. The Berglas-Razin point is, of course, valid for the HOS model, but it would not apply if a specific-factor model were used, which may be more appropriate for short-run analysis.[21]

Third, there is the question of the terms of trade among traded commodities. For present purposes, all that is important is to note that the terms of trade can be affected by an exchange-rate change or by a change in the nominal money stocks in a world (two-country) model with home goods, traded goods, and money, although the composite-commodity theorem can no longer be invoked. Recall that in response to an exogenous devaluation, home consumers reduce real expenditures (to restore real cash balances at the higher price level prevailing after devaluation), whereas foreigners increase real spending to reduce their cash balances. The demand for the tradable goods produced in the home country shifts downward by an amount equal to the home country's marginal propensity to spend on its own tradable goods times the reduction in expenditure. The demand for its tradable goods shifts upward by an amount

[21] See Jones (1971) for an exposition of the specific-factor model.

equal to the foreign country's marginal propensity to spend on the home country's tradable goods times its increase in expenditure. Because the reduction in expenditure in one country equals the increase in the other country, whether or not there is any change in the terms of trade depends on whether or not there is a difference in marginal propensities to spend on traded goods.[22]

There is no theoretical presumption as to the sign of any difference in marginal propensities to spend. Indeed, if there is a presumption at all, it is probably that they are much the same.[23] But if they are different, there can be changes in relative prices among tradables. Whether the terms of trade improve or deteriorate depends simply on those differences in marginal propensities.

If the terms of trade do change, however, there will, in general, be feedback on the hoarding functions.[24] Thus, the "impact" effect of devaluation via the changed desired levels of hoarding can be augmented by the effect on desired levels of real cash balances of any terms-of-trade change. For that reason, it cannot be asserted that the expenditure effects of devaluation are separate from the relative price effects. In the case in which marginal propensities to spend on tradable goods differ, there will be an interaction between relative price changes and desired real cash balances.

[22] The analysis proceeds similarly in terms of the foreign country's tradable goods. Because the sum of the three marginal propensities to spend (home goods, home country's tradable goods, and foreign country's tradable goods) equals unity, and because expenditure changes on home goods equal changes in income in the home-goods sector, a higher marginal propensity to spend on the home country's goods implies a lower marginal propensity to spend on the foreign country's goods.

[23] See the exchange between Jones (1970) and Samuelson (1971) on this issue.

[24] See Dornbusch (1973a) for an elaboration of the model.

4

Models of the capital account

Perhaps because financial capital flows were generally so restricted in the first two decades after World War II, the theory of exchange-rate adjustment and the balance of payments was largely confined to analyses of the current account. When Mundell, Johnson, and others began espousing the "monetary approach to the balance of payments," one major source of misunderstanding was that many economists, accustomed to thinking in terms of current-account transactions, understood them to be discussing determinants of exports and imports of goods and services.

Partly because of earlier neglect, most of the work on exchange-rate determination and the balance of payments in the past ten years has focused, one way or another, on the capital account. Indeed, in the mid-1970s, a reader of the literature might well have been forgiven had he assumed that all international transactions consisted of capital flows! Only in the past few years has attention begun to focus on links between current-account and capital-account determinants, the role of expectations, and so on.

In this chapter, models that focus primarily on capital-account transactions are reviewed. It remains for Chapter 5 to examine links between current account and capital account. Section 4.1 introduces the monetary approach to the balance of payments as it was developed by the mid-1970s. Section 4.2 gives the dynamic version of the monetary approach that arises when it is assumed that goods-market adjustments are not instantaneous. Section 4.3 then proceeds to portfolio and asset-market approaches to analyses of exchange-rate determination and the balance of payments.

Three preliminary observations are in order. First and foremost, emphasis on the capital account has inevitably focused attention on stock-adjustment and stock-flow-adjustment models. In so doing, there has naturally been a tendency to link modern monetary theory more closely with the theory of exchange-rate and balance-of-payments determination than was formerly the case. Given the extent to which modern monetary theory is itself in a state of flux, it would be surprising if efforts to incorporate that theory into open-economy models did not reflect that fact, and indeed they do.

Second, because the models are primarily of a stock-adjustment variety, they are usually characterized by the distinction between momentary equilibrium (in which individuals carry out their desired transactions as a function of their initial holdings) and steady-state equilibrium (in which initial desired stocks equal initial holdings, so that there is no change in stocks over time).

Third, the major source of the apparent differences among the models reviewed here hinges on assumptions – often implicit – about the degree of substitutability between various classes of domestic and foreign assets, on the one hand, and the speed of adjustment in different markets, on the other. In principle, there are six asset markets: domestic and foreign currency, domestic and foreign bonds, and domestic and foreign equities. Whenever any combinations of these are perfect substitutes, they can be aggregated, using the composite-commodity theorem. Whenever there is no substitutability (as, for example, if foreigners cannot hold domestic bonds), then use of the small-country assumption can reduce still further the number of markets with which the analyst must deal.

4.1 The monetary approach to the balance of payments

The monetary approach to the balance of payments represents the intellectual bridge between the earlier, current-account models of the 1960s and the modern understanding of the crucial variables in exchange-rate determination. Although recent models go well beyond the insights of the monetary approach, it was sufficiently important in shifting thought that it deserves elaboration here.

The approach originated in the work of a group of economists, primarily teaching at or trained at the University of Chicago, led by Robert Mundell and Harry G. Johnson. That work had been preceded by the work of J. J. Polak and others at the International Monetary Fund in the late 1950s and early 1960s.[1] Prais (1961) and Kemp (1962) had earlier provided models capturing the essential features of the monetary stock-flow-adjustment process that were surprisingly neglected by the profession.

In its original development, the monetary approach generally lumped together current-account and private capital-account transactions and focused on the determinants of the official settlements balance under fixed exchange rates. That in itself was a major shift in the focus of exchange-rate and balance-of-payments theory, because the current account was no longer regarded as the major focal point.

It is simplest to approach the topic by setting forth the components of the monetary approach as it was understood and exposited in the early 1970s (for simplicity, referred to as the 1974 model).[2] That model has since been extended and

---

[1] See Frenkel (1976) for an examination of the history of thought on monetary approaches to analysis of the balance of payments and exchange-rate determination.

[2] The year 1974 was used as a "characteristic" year for the original monetary approach because 1975 saw the publication of the important Frenkel-Rodriguez article, which provided the first systematic treatment of asset accumulation and current-account determination within the monetary-approach framework. The extension was a breakthrough of sufficient importance to shift the entire focus of

amended in a variety of ways, so that at the present time it is difficult to distinguish an adherent of the monetary approach from the author of a portfolio-balance model, as discussed in Section 4.3. Indeed, there probably remain no adherents to the 1974 model in its simple form.[3]

The fundamental contribution of the monetary-approach theorists was to recognize and emphasize the stock-flow-adjustment nature of the determinants of the balance of payments under fixed exchange rates or of the exchange rate under flexible rates. Under fixed rates, emphasis was on the determinants of the balance of payments, defined as the "official settlements balance" – the change in the international monetary holdings of the monetary authority. As Johnson (1977, p. 259) emphasized repeatedly:

> The purpose of the "monetary approach" is to develop a theory of the balance of payments based on the fact that the balance of payments is a monetary phenomenon in a monetary international economy, and requires analysis in terms of monetary concepts, and especially the concept of money as a stock and of monetary adjustments as adjustments of actual to desired stocks, rather than in terms of international money flows as the residuals of "real" flows determined by real relative prices and incomes.

In this formulation, the balance-of-payments deficit (at a fixed exchange rate) is seen as the means by which a country's citizens rid themselves of an excess supply of money: By Walras's law, such an excess (stock) supply of money is reflected in a flow reduction in the money stock (the stock-flow-adjustment pro-

---

analysis, bringing it much closer to the portfolio-balance approach espoused by Branson and others.

[3] By 1980, labels were hopelessly confused, as some developers of the monetary approach continued to label their models as such despite the fact that there were strong elements of portfolio balance in them. For critiques of the 1974 model, see Corden (1977, Chapter 3) and Whitman (1975).

cess), the counterpart of which must be the excess of the value
of goods, services, and assets imported into the country over the
value exported, measured at the prevailing exchange rate.

In most formulations, the 1974 model was set against the
background of a fully employed economy in which perfect com-
petition was assumed to prevail in all markets, with full price
and wage flexibility.[4] Perhaps the simplest specification, in the
fixed-exchange-rate case, is for a small country facing a large
international trading world. Then the following five equations
describe the system for the home country:

$$M^d = PK(Y) \tag{4.1}$$
$$P = EP^* \tag{4.2}$$
$$M^s \equiv D + R \cdot E \tag{4.3}$$
$$\dot{R} \equiv (M^d - M^s)/E \tag{4.4}$$
$$\dot{R} \equiv B \tag{4.5}$$

where E is the fixed price of foreign currency per unit of domestic currency, P^* is the foreign price level (exogenously given),
P is the domestic price level, Y is domestic real income, D is the
quantity of domestic credit, and R is the quantity of reserves
measured in units of foreign currency. M^d and M^s are the quantities of money demanded and supplied. Equation (4.3), the
money supply, is an identity. $\dot{X}$ denotes the instantaneous rate
of change in the variable X.

Equation (4.1) is a conventional demand-for-money relation
as a function of the price level and real income (determined by
the supply side of the system and therefore exogenous to the
model).[5]

Equation (4.2) is the purchasing-power-parity equation,
which will be discussed in Section 4.1.1. Given the exogenous

---

[4] For representative expositions, see the collections of studies in
Frenkel and Johnson (1976, 1978) and Bilson (1979).
[5] See Section 4.1.2 for a discussion of the role of the interest rate. It
is omitted here to make the exposition consistent with current practice and the monetary approach. Implicitly, money is the only
asset.

price level and the exchange rate, the domestic price level is determined. This, in turn, determines the level of the money stock individuals wish to hold.

Equation (4.3) defines the money supply as equal to the supply of domestic credit plus the quantity of reserves held by the monetary authority. In essence, this equation has built into it the important assumption that the monetary authority either cannot or does not sterilize at all changes in reserve holdings.

These three equations are sufficient to establish a monetary equilibrium: Given initial D and R, the supply of money is given. Given the exogenously determined price level (via the exchange rate and foreign price level), the demand for money as a stock is given. The difference between demand and supply is the change in reserves, as stated in equation (4.4), which gives the law of motion of the system. Starting from an initial position of, say, excess supply of money, reserves decrease. As they do, the reserve component of the domestic money supply contracts, thus diminishing the gap between demand and supply. A steady state occurs when $\dot{R}$ is zero, so that initially held balances are desired balances at prevailing prices.

Note that equations (4.1) through (4.4) describe the entire process as one of monetary adjustment. Equation (4.5) simply adds another variable: the balance of payments. It defines the change in reserves as equal to the value of the balance of payments.

Several comments are in order. First and foremost, B is not a definition of the current-account surplus or deficit. B is defined as the sum of the current-account and capital-account transactions other than those of the monetary authority. Second, price flexibility is assumed to prevail in all markets so that the monetary model has no real effects. Third, note the implicit assumption that adjustment is costless and that individuals can carry out their desired transactions instantaneously. Hence, it is assumed that any excess stock of money is immediately reflected in a net inflow of goods and assets of equal magnitude.

Fourth, incorporation of a second country into the model,

with endogenous determination of the world price level, is no† difficult. Add a second money-demand equation for the second country and also the requirement that the sum of money demands (with that of the second country valued in terms of the first country's currency at the fixed exchange rate) equal the sum of world reserves plus the two supplies of domestic credi† (valued in terms of the first country's currency). Given the exchange rate, there is one price level for the home country that will satisfy the equation. That then determines the second country's price level. These solutions can then be used to solve for each country's change in reserves.[6] From there on out, the model works through time, as described for the single country. with the price levels in each country constant after full equilibrium is reached.

Fifth, the essentially transitory effect of devaluation on the balance of payments is clearly seen in this model. Because the impact effect of an exchange-rate change is on the demand for nominal balances, the devaluing country's residents attempt to restore their real cash balances by reducing their expenditures: there will thus be an excess of income over expenditures and an inflow of reserves. The country whose currency has appreciated. by contrast, will initially have a real money supply above desired levels; hence, residents will spend in excess of income to run down cash balances.[7]

Thus, the reasoning goes, any devaluation (from an initial stock equilibrium) will generate a temporary surplus in the balance of payments as domestic residents increase their nominal balances. However, once they have done so, full equilibrium will be restored. One can, of course, ask this question: Why, if the

---

[6] The two changes must sum to zero, or otherwise the sum of money demands will not equal the sum of money supplies.

[7] The exact division of price-level changes between the devaluing country and the rest of the world is a function of the sizes of the countries; for present purposes, it suffices to assert that the price level will rise (but by less than the proportion of devaluation) in the devaluing country and fall in the rest of the world, also by less than in proportion to the exchange-rate appreciation.

initial position was one of full equilibrium, would a country devalue? The answer emanating from the monetary approach would have to be that domestic credit creation had earlier run down reserves and that devaluation, by lowering real balances, would induce hoarding and an increase in reserves.

Sixth, it should be noted that the assumption that the monetary authority cannot sterilize reserves is critical. That this assumption might be reasonable was put forth in an important article by Kouri and Porter (1974), who questioned the degree to which the monetary authorities could influence the money supply through their actions. They argued that, instead, "capital flows are to a large part the result of changes in monetary policy, as reflected in changes in the net domestic assets of the Central Bank and the required reserves" (p. 464). Although Kouri and Porter argued that there was a large offset to domestic monetary actions, they did not conclude that it was perfect. For the early proponents of the monetary approach, however, the money supply became a totally endogenous variable, with the only choice variable for the monetary authorities being the composition of money as between reserves and domestic credit.

Finally, the insights of the monetary approach in the form reflected in equations (4.1) through (4.5) were used to explain the stylized fact that countries experiencing more rapid rates of growth of real output were also the countries in the 1950s and 1960s that appeared to have chronic tendencies toward balance-of-payments surpluses at more or less fixed exchange rates. The reasoning was that higher rates of growth of real income generate higher rates of growth of demand for real balances. What was not explained was why rapidly growing countries' monetary authorities did not commensurately increase the rate of growth of the domestic credit base.

The basic model presented earlier can readily cover the case of flexible exchange rates. The system can be written

$$M = PK(Y) \tag{4.6}$$
$$M^* = P^*K(Y^*) \tag{4.7}$$

$E = \text{domestic} / \text{foreign}$

$$P = EP^* \tag{4.8}$$

$$E = \frac{MK(Y^*)}{M^*K(Y)} \tag{4.9}$$

where, for simplicity, the demand-for-money functions, K, are taken to be the same in both countries. Equation (4.6) repeats equation (4.1); equation (4.7) is the same for the second country (rest of the world). Equation (4.8) repeats equation (4.2). Equation (4.9) is derived by substituting (4.6) and (4.7) into (4.8), with E taken as endogenous to the system, and M and M^* assumed given. In this model there are no changes in reserves; the exchange rate adjusts to clear the money market in each country.

It is in this form that the claim made by Frenkel (1976), Mussa (1976), and others in the 1974 model is most clearly seen: The exchange rate was said to be the relative price of two monies.[8] From (4.9), an increase in M leads to an increase in the price of foreign exchange, whereas an increase in M^*, the foreign country's money supply, leads to a reduction. Note further that for given interest rates and real incomes, the rate of home-currency depreciation equals the difference in the rate of monetary growth.

Three linkages are essential to the 1974 model, and they play important roles in all modern models of exchange-rate or balance-of-payments determination. First and foremost, there is the purchasing-power-parity (PPP) relation, indicated in equa-

---

[8] See Section 4.2.3 for a discussion of currency-substitution models. It should be noted that the exchange rate is the price of one currency in terms of another, by definition. What was meant by the monetary-approach theorists was something stronger than that, however, in that they were implying a degree of causation between money supplies and exchange rates that does not follow from the definition. As Elhanan Helpman pointed out in conversation, one could as easily take two countries' holdings of bonds (in their own currencies) and define the exchange rate as the relative price of bonds, or take their national incomes in their own currencies and define the exchange rate as the price of a unit of income in one country relative to that in another.

tion (4.8). Under fixed exchange rates, so the argument goes, the law of one price assures that the domestic price level is determined by the exchange rate.[9] The monetary authority is powerless, except in the short run, to alter the money supply; any creation of domestic credit will be offset by an outflow of reserves. Under flexible exchange rates, the money supply can be altered by the monetary authority, but the exchange rate then adjusts to determine a price level at which individuals will be willing to hold the money supply. Because of its crucial role in this analysis, as well as in linking current account and capital account in ways to be discussed in Chapter 5, PPP will be discussed in Section 4.1.1. The second linkage, also important for later models as well as this one, is the link between the spot and forward exchange rates, and therefore between interest rates in the home country and the rest of the world. That relation, along with the Fisher equation linking nominal and real interest rates and rates of inflation across countries, will be taken up in Section 4.1.2. Section 4.1.3 will then show how these linkages generate the model of equations (4.1) through (4.5) or (4.6) through (4.9).

4.1.1 *Purchasing-power parity*

In one sense, questions surrounding PPP and its interpretation are central to the theory of exchange-rate determination. If one asks what determines the exchange rate, a first step might be to separate out the nominal and real components of that determination. Ideally, one would hope that the theory of exchange-rate determination for a small country (given world prices) might be of the (reduced) form

$$E_t = P_t f(x_1, x_2, \ldots, x_n; t) \qquad (4.10)$$

where E_t is the nominal exchange rate at time t, P_t is some index of the domestic price level, and $x_1, \ldots, x_n$ are real variables. If one could formulate the theory in that form, then $E_t/$

---

[9] This is the continuous version of PPP (see Section 4.1.1).

P_t would be the "real exchange rate," and $x_1, x_2, \ldots, x_n$ and time could be analyzed as to their effects on the real exchange rate.

To be sure, a relation such as (4.10) implies a dichotomy of the influence of nominal and real components, and a prior question is whether or not such a separation is warranted.[10] It will be seen in Section 4.2 that one can construct a model in which the real exchange rate alters over time in response to nominal shocks, so that the time argument may be of importance. In another context, Helpman and Razin (1981) have modeled the behavior of the real exchange rate over time as a function of differences among countries in rates of time preference (see Sections 5.2 and 5.3).

For present purposes, however, there is another interpretation of (4.10). In its strongest form, PPP as a theorem can be interpreted as saying that the f function takes on a value of unity for all equilibria. In that strong version, in the monetary approach to the balance of payments, the PPP theorem says that for a small country, a fixed exchange rate determines the domestic price level, whereas under a flexible exchange rate the domestic price level (determined by the money supply) determines the exchange rate. It was in this form that the 1974 model used the PPP theorem, and it is this viewpoint that underlies advocacy of fixed exchange rates by Mundell and others.[11]

In another sense, however, it is very unclear what all the fuss over PPP is about. Equation (4.10) as written does not state that domestic prices times the exchange rate equal foreign prices; it could well be that P_t is an index of the price of home goods and that as long as the f function is unity (or its arguments taking

---

[10] In many models, it might follow from the first-order homogeneity of the behavioral relations in nominal variables and zero-degree homogeneity of real variables.

[11] There is another interpretation of a relation such as (4.10) that can yield the monetary-approach results. It might be asserted that the x's are all exogenous and are not subject to policy decisions. In that event, the same conclusions would hold as if the f function were always unity.

on constant values), the implications will be much the same as strict PPP (with a constant foreign price level).

Nonetheless, the literature on PPP is vast, and it is important if only because it has attracted so much attention. As set forth in equation (4.2), the proposition that "the" domestic price in domestic currency equals "the" foreign price in foreign currency times the exchange rate appears straightforward.[12] On closer examination, however, it is not entirely evident what is meant. In a one-commodity model, one could invoke arbitrage and either a zero-transport-cost assumption or a constant-transport-cost (with no time lags) assumption to ensure that equation (4.2) would always hold.[13] But the meaning of PPP as a theory of exchange-rate determination is not at all clear.

In a many-commodity model, the meaning is less clear. After the fact, with perfect costless arbitrage and no transport costs, PPP might hold for each traded commodity. Whether or not under flexible exchange rates this implies that prices of all commodities will be equalized with their counterpart foreign prices, or whether the exchange rate determines prices or prices determine exchange rates, is another matter. Moreover, there are questions as to whether PPP should be interpreted as a short-run or a long-run equilibrium condition or as an identity. The literature, both analytical and empirical, has mushroomed over

---

[12] Elhanan Helpman pointed out in conversation that it makes little difference conceptually whether one writes $E = P/P^*$ or $E = W/W^*$, where W is the nominal wage rate in units of domestic currency and the asterisks denote foreign variables, or $E = Y/Y^*$, where Y is GNP in domestic currency.

[13] In such models, the only international trade is the exchange of goods for assets. One then derives conditions about steady-state rates of flow of assets in one direction and goods in the other as a function of differences in rates of time preferences between populations. Kareken and Wallace (1977) have provided such a model, and the interested reader should consult it. It should be noted that overlapping-generations models are really addressed to analyzing determinants of the components of the balance of payments – capital account and current account – rather than to the exchange rate or the deficit in the balance of payments.

the past decade because of its central importance in the monetary-approach models.[14]

The short-term empirical evidence of the 1970s does not lend support to a PPP hypothesis in any of its forms, and the longer-term evidence is open to a number of interpretations.[15] If, in fact, there had been overwhelming empirical evidence in favor of one version or another of PPP, it is doubtful that the discussion would have been so extended. Much of the analysis takes on the appearance of a phenomenon in search of a theory, as authors either have found reasons why PPP fails to hold (poor data, wrong measures, etc.) or have developed alternative versions of PPP. Some authors, such as Dornbusch (1980*a*), provided tables setting forth divergences in rates of price increases and exchange-rate movements during the 1970s and concluded that PPP did not work well in either the short run or the long run. Others, notably Frenkel (1980*a*), applied regression analysis to monthly data from the floating-rate periods of the 1920s and the 1970s and demonstrated that PPP performed much better in the 1920s.[16]

"Absolute" PPP has been interpreted to mean that price levels are equated between countries, whereas "relative" PPP is the prediction that the proportionate change in the home country's price level is equal to the proportionate change in the product of the foreign price level and the exchange rate.[17] Either

---

[14] See Katseli (1979) for a survey.

[15] See Isard (1977), the survey by Officer (1976), and the *Journal of International Economics* symposium on the subject in the May 1978 issue.

[16] Even if PPP did hold, that would not necessarily provide useful information for analysis of a devaluation or of exchange-rate determination. Suppose, for example, a two-country, two-good model in which each country specializes in the production of one commodity. Let each monetary authority stabilize the price of the domestically produced good. Even with perfect arbitrage (and therefore with PPP holding, with the same weights used to form the price index in each country), the fact that PPP will always hold provides no useful information about the impact of a devaluation. It should be noted that the model just sketched may not be compatible with equilibrium at more than one exchange rate.

[17] Fama and Farber (1979) have shown that PPP and frictionless international capital markets imply the same real return on a secu-

version can be interpreted (1) as a prediction of exchange-rate movements, given rates of inflation, (2) as an equilibrium condition, or (3) as an identity holding for tradable goods and services (Samuelson, 1966).

It should be noted that absolute PPP can hold even in the presence of home goods. This could occur if home goods and tradables were sufficiently close substitutes in production, or it could occur if trade assured factor price equalization and the technologies for producing home goods were identical. There are two possible time horizons for which PPP might hold: One is the long run; under this, the short-run exchange rate tends toward a long-run equilibrium that is PPP.[18] Short-run fluctuations in the exchange rate can occur for a variety of reasons[19] (presumably as a function of a disturbance in the underlying parameters of the system), but once such a disturbance has occurred, the exchange rate eventually returns to its long-run PPP rate. The alternative stricter version is that PPP must always hold, even in the short run.

Yet another issue pertains to the question whether or not PPP is the sole determinant of exchange rates. Marina Whitman (1975) has distinguished "global monetarism" from the monetary approach to the balance of payments by noting that the former view holds that the world economy is one integrated market, that world prices and the exchange rate determine domestic price, and that the integration of the world economy (including capital flow) assures that a change in the exchange rate can do nothing other than alter the domestic price level. By contrast, the 1974 model conceded that exchange rates could influence "real" variables in the short run, but asserted that the resulting increases or decreases in the money supply (given the

---

rity or commodity for residents of all countries, regardless of different risks of inflation in different countries.

[18] See Section 4.2, in which PPP is the long-run-equilibrium exchange rate under exchange-rate-dynamics models.

[19] In Chapter 5 it will be seen that PPP expectations can validate a rational-expectations model of exchange-rate determination and simultaneously bring the current-account variables back into prominence in those models.

inability or unwillingness of the monetary authority to offset changes in official balances) would continue until PPP was validated as a steady-state equilibrium relationship once again.

It is possible to take a milder approach, which Officer (1976) associated with Cassel,[20] and which has recently been reinforced by the work of Darby (1980). That is, all else being held equal, a monetary disturbance will generate price-level and/or exchange-rate changes that will result in the restoration of the original PPP relationship. In this form, it is conceded that factors other than "equality of purchasing power" may influence the equilibrium real exchange rate, but if rates of inflation diverge between countries while other arguments of the exchange-rate function are constant, the rate of change in the exchange rate will (tend to?) equal the rate of divergence. For example, a change in a country's terms of trade might warrant a change in the "real" exchange rate (i.e., in the relation between domestic and foreign prices). Such a possibility is not inconsistent with the view that as long as the terms of trade (and other underlying real variables) are unchanged, the time path of the exchange rate will follow the differential in inflation rates between the country and the rest of the world.[21] Darby (1980) presented results that are consistent with this interpretation and noted that research on the underlying causes of permanent shifts in the real exchange rate is needed.[22]

It is at this juncture in the argument that issues arise as to the appropriate price index and also as to other determinants of

---

[20] But see Samuelson's interpretation (1966), which rejects the view that Cassel held that particular form of PPP.

[21] McKinnon seems to have taken this view, noting that PPP works best in explaining exchange-rate changes between countries with very different rates of inflation (McKinnon, 1979, pp. 127–8). However, Dornbusch concluded that "most students of PPP conclude that the theory does not hold up to the facts except in a very loose and approximate fashion" (Dornbusch, 1980*b*).

[22] Darby (1980) also noted that the prediction errors of the relative PPP formulation become smaller the longer the time horizon, whereas those of the absolute formulation become larger.

the exchange rate. The monetary-disturbance hypothesis is essentially an extension of the Patinkin dichotomy: If the money supply doubles, prices will double, with all real variables in the system unaffected. It shares with the dichotomy all the issues in macroeconomics pertaining to short-run and long-run adjustments. Frenkel has shown that the failure of PPP to hold in the 1970s as well as it did in the 1920s was, at least in part, related to the wider divergences between wholesale and consumer price indices within countries in the 1970s. He interpreted the differences in these two indices to reflect, at least in large measure, changes in relative prices between tradable and nontradable goods. In response to these shifts in relative prices, it is not evident what the PPP prediction is.[23]

There are few theories as to determinants of the exchange rate other than PPP. The exchange-rate-overshooting model predicts short-term deviations from PPP. And, as mentioned earlier, Helpman and Razin (1981) focused on different rates of time preferences. Another line of reasoning is really based on empirical observation. It is the systematic tendency, identified by Balassa (1964) and documented by Kravis and Lipsey (1978), for the real exchange rate to appreciate with rising per-capita incomes. Although some PPP advocates have asserted that international linkages of traded-goods prices would be sufficient to keep home-goods prices much the same across countries, Balassa and Samuelson assumed that home goods tend to be labor-intensive and, as such, to be cheaper in countries with lower real wage levels. Hence, home goods would tend to be relatively cheaper in countries with lower per-capita incomes. The testable hypothesis that results is that the purchasing power of a unit of currency (translated at the equilibrium exchange rate) should be greater in countries with lower per-capita

---

[23] Because tradables have greater weight in wholesale prices than in consumer prices, the divergence between the two indices may increase with the importance of trade in GNP. It is questionable whether or not that is independent of departures from PPP.

incomes.[24] The work of Kravis, Kennessey, Heston, and Summers (1974) has documented that this does, indeed, tend to be the case. However, there remain significant questions as to whether or not differences in purchasing power of the magnitude reported by these authors can be explained in terms of differences in home-goods prices.[25]

Finally, there is the point that one could have all prices equalized between countries at every moment, and yet observe differences in recorded rates of increases in price indices if index weights differed. At first glance, the point seems trivial and obvious, but it has important ramifications for empirical analysis of PPP theories: Because price levels are never directly comparable across countries, what is usually observed is price indices.[26] In this form, it makes a significant difference whether a cost-of-living price index, a wholesale price index, an index of home-goods prices (almost never available), or some other measure of the price level is used. Not only is it possible that rates of increase might diverge among these indices, they in fact do, often by considerable amounts. Although there is no theoretically correct answer as to what index should be used (because one can formulate different PPP theories, and the appropriate index can vary with the theory), it should be noted that, in general, an index that gives heavy weight to traded goods does not provide a fair test of the absolute version of the PPP theory.[27]

[24] It should be noted that this discussion presumes that one observes (or knows of periods in the past when one could have observed) equilibrium exchange rates. In the PPP literature, there has been little attention to defining an equilibrium rate. By contrast, under exchange-control regimes, all observers have concluded that long periods may have contained no observation of an equilibrium rate, and there is a large literature as to how to identify one. This matter will be discussed in Chapter 8.

[25] Officer (1976) explored the question whether or not some of the observed differences might arise because of quality differentials in goods and services. See the exchange between Balassa (1974) and Officer (1974) on this issue.

[26] An important exception is the work of Kravis et al. (1974).

[27] But see Isard (1977) and Kravis and Lipsey (1978), who challenged the view that prices of tradable goods are internationally equalized.

In general, there are sound analytical reasons for skepticism about the proposition that PPP must hold, in either its absolute or relative form, without qualification. Qualification may be with respect to the time dimension, or it may be with respect to holding other factors constant. Despite these observations, it nonetheless remains the case that most economists, if informed that rates of inflation in the United States and Brazil differed by 60 percent annually, would predict that the Brazilian price of foreign exchange would rise by about 60 percent per year. To be sure, likely future trends in coffee prices, real wages, and so on might qualify the forecast, but as many have noted, fluctuations in real variables of the order of magnitude of inflation differentials are seldom observed for sustained periods of time.[28]

4.1.2 *Interest rates and forward exchange rates*

The reader will have observed that the demand for money, as represented in (4.1) and (4.6), was not assumed to be a function of the interest rate. Omitting the interest rate can be justified by assuming, as did the monetary-approach theorists, that there is an internationally integrated capital market, with the domestic interest rate determined by the international rate. If that is the case, the composite-commodity theorem tells us that domestic and foreign bonds can be treated as a single asset. If it is further assumed that portfolio adjustment is instantaneous and costless, desired and actual bond holdings will be equal at each instant of time. Hence, the instantaneous change in reserves will equal the instantaneous change in the difference between increased money demand and increased supply.[29]

---

[28] McKinnon (1979) concluded that "until a more robust theory replaces it, I shall assume that purchasing power parity among tradable goods tends to hold in the long run in the absence of overt impediments to trade and among countries with convertible currencies" (p. 136).

[29] If interest rates are included in the demand-for-money function, then, logically, wealth must also be included. If, as the interest rate

It is the treatment of interest rates as being internationally determined that most sharply separates the 1974 monetary approach from the portfolio-balance approach discussed in Section 4.3. The PPP theorem, combined with the theory of forward exchange, provides the analytical underpinning for the monetary approach, assuming a zero rate of expected inflation. When the expected rate of inflation is positive, the Fisher equation (to be discussed later) must be added to the system.

The theory of forward exchange is integral to the monetary approach. Its initial formulation is generally credited to Keynes, and it was well known in the Bretton Woods years. Its main use was as a defense against critics of flexible exchange rates who argued that floating rates would increase the risk associated with international transactions. In refutation of that assertion, the proposition that forward markets would permit traders to guard against exchange risk was advanced.

Beginning in the 1970s, the fact that exchange rates have been flexible and the fact that a forward market has existed have produced renewed interest in the theory of forward exchange. Interest has intensified because exchange rates have displayed what has been to many observers a surprisingly great degree of volatility. Simultaneous with the emergence of a set of observations ripe for empirical analysis, recognition of the function of exchange rates vis-à-vis asset markets has heightened analysts' awareness of the role of expectations as a determinant of the future course of exchange rates. Here we shall review the basic theory and indicate its role in the monetary approach to the balance of payments.

Essentially, the theory of forward exchange rates (also sometimes referred to as interest-rate parity) is based on the propo-

changes, the desired quantity of money held changes, there must be a changing composition of wealth holding. Thus, wealth must be included as an argument in the demand-for-money function if the interest rate is included. Prais (1961) first provided this formulation. I am indebted to Elhanan Helpman for helpful discussions on this point.

sition that in the absence of transaction costs, the premium (i.e., the proportionate differential between the forward and spot exchange rates) must equal the interest-rate differential (measured over the same time interval). The reason for this is that one could risklessly (at least with regard to exchange risk) buy foreign bonds and sell foreign exchange forward. Should the premium fall short of the interest-rate differential, it would pay investors to buy foreign bonds and sell domestic bonds. Should the premium exceed the differential, the converse incentives would hold. Therefore, only when the premium equals the interest differential can there exist an equilibrium in the bond market. Formally,

$$\frac{F}{E} = \frac{1 + i}{1 + i^*} \qquad \left(f - e = i - i^* \right) \text{ logs} \qquad (4.11)$$

where E is the spot price of foreign currency, F is the forward price of foreign currency, i is the domestic interest rate, and i^* is the foreign interest rate. If transactions costs are negligible and political and default risks are ignored, arbitragers can earn a profit whenever equation (4.11) is not satisfied.

As it stands, equation (4.11) is an equilibrium condition that states a relationship that must hold between interest-rate differentials and the spot and forward exchange rates. It indicates nothing about the determinants of any particular variable until more flesh is placed on the model, although it does serve as a useful reminder that countries' monetary authorities cannot follow interest-rate targets and simultaneously attempt to regulate the forward exchange rate under a fixed-exchange-rate system.[30] Indeed, it points out that intervention in the forward market can be equivalent to domestic open-market operations for a small country: Intervention in the forward exchange market must alter the domestic rate of interest, and open-market

---

[30] If the exchange rate is fixed and a country is sufficiently small that the world interest rate is given, E and i^* must move together, as is readily seen from equation (4.11).

operations affecting the domestic rate of interest must also lead to an alteration in the premium on forward exchange.[31]

We already have, from equation (4.11), that the forward–spot relationship must satisfy the interest-rate-differential condition. Suppose, however, that speculators believe that the rate of depreciation of the home currency will exceed the forward discount. Then presumably they will buy spot foreign exchange, selling forward. The converse will happen if expectations are for appreciation of the home currency. Thus, through arbitrage (and in the absence of risk-aversion), we expect that the premium on forward exchange will reflect the expected rate of currency depreciation. Hence, a second relationship between the spot rate and the forward rate must, under these assumptions, be

$$E^e = F \tag{4.12}$$

where E^e is the expected future spot rate and F is the forward rate. Equation (4.12) is used as a basis for asserting that the forward rate is the best predictor of the future exchange rate.[32]

Neither equation alone, nor both together, can provide a complete model of exchange-rate (or interest-rate) determination. An oil well discovered off the coast of Mexico might alter expectations and affect the spot rate and the forward rate. Assuming that interest-rate and inflation-rate expectations are not affected (a questionable assumption made here only for expository purposes), the adjustment mechanism might well be that speculators will buy forward pesos and sell forward dollars. Any widening of the forward–spot relationship will immediately induce covered-interest arbitrage as arbitragers shift into peso-denominated assets. This upward shift in the demand for

---

[31] There is a literature dealing with reasons why the interest-parity theorem might not hold. Aliber (1973) has argued that political risk – the probability that the authorities will impose controls – is a factor. See Dooley and Isard (1980) for a recent analysis.

[32] See Levich (1979*a*,*b*) and Bilson (1980) for a survey of the large and rapidly growing literature associated with the analysis and testing of this proposition.

pesos (downward shift in the demand for dollars) naturally leads to an appreciation of the spot exchange rate for the peso. Whether the realignment of exchange rates arises primarily because of speculation (and thus the behavior of the future rate) or because of arbitrage is not specified by this model as it stands, and thus the behavior of the spot rate is not specified in the equilibrium conditions (4.11) and (4.12).[33]

Finally, there is the Fisher equation. As is well known, the Fisher equation simply states that the real rate of interest is equal to the nominal rate of interest less the expected rate of inflation. If real rates of interest are equalized throughout the world through capital mobility, then nominal-interest-rate differentials must reflect differences in expected inflation rates. Formally,

$$i = r + \pi, \quad i^* = r + \pi^* \tag{4.13}$$

where r is the real interest rate, assumed equalized throughout the world, and π is the expected inflation rate, assumed specific to each country. The Fisher equation, combined with PPP and the forward–spot relation, provides the underpinning of the 1974 model.

4.1.3 *Combining the three relations*

Suppose now a neoclassical world, consisting of two countries, in each of which the usual competitive conditions are met. Assume further that future inflation rates are known with certainty. Then, from equation (4.13), the difference in future rates of inflation equals the difference in nominal interest rates. From (4.11), this difference must equal the forward–spot differential. But, from (4.12), the forward rate is the expected future spot rate.

---

[33] Moreover, as should be evident, the fact that expectations would induce an increased capital inflow (reduced capital outflow) into Mexico is clear evidence that the interest rate might reasonably be expected to alter as part of the adjustment process. See the discussion of exchange-rate dynamics in Section 4.2.

That reasoning, in turn, implies that expectations formation via the PPP theorem provides a rational-expectations model of exchange-rate determination.[34] Indeed, given equations (4.11), (4.12), and (4.13), there can be no rational-expectations solution other than PPP consistent with those equilibrium conditions. For, as can easily be seen, PPP is implied by the model.

Hence, PPP is seen as the long-run anchor for exchange rates. Under flexible exchange rates, different rates of monetary expansion in different countries generate different nominal interest rates and a spot–forward exchange-rate relationship that equals the expected difference in the inflation rate; that, in turn, is consistent with PPP. Should one country then alter its expected rate of money creation, covered-interest arbitrage plus speculation will ensure that the spot and forward exchange rates will both adjust instantaneously to the newly anticipated time paths.[35]

As Hahn (1977) noted in his review of the Frenkel-Johnson book, the real-world assumptions underlying the 1974 model in this form are those of a frictionless, costless, instantaneous-adjustment world. Resources are allocated efficiently, and real output is determined by neoclassical forces. Monetary variables have no impact on the real variables of the system. Capital is perfectly mobile internationally.

The great contribution of the monetary approach in this form was to shift attention to asset markets and to develop a stock-flow framework for analysis of exchange-rate determination

---

[34] This result was initially due to Kouri (1976). It is, of course, possible that the price weights used for PPP are different than those applicable to domestic expenditure (e.g., the nominal–real interest differential might be based on the expected rate of increase of the consumer price index, whereas PPP expectations were based on expected behavior of the wholesale price index).

[35] Under fixed exchange rates, rates of inflation must be expected to be the same throughout the world. Should one country's monetary authority set out to increase the money supply at a rate (as contrasted with a once-and-for-all increase) above the world rate of inflation, the model will be inconsistent: The exchange rate cannot remain fixed.

and balance-of-payments adjustment. Its lasting contribution, beyond that fundamental insight and the later research it stimulated, probably lies in the analysis of determinants of long-run steady-state equilibrium. Indeed, as will be seen, most asset-market models and most of the recent work linking current-account and capital-account behavior retain some form of the PPP, spot–forward rate linkage, and Fisher-equation relations as the underlying determinants of long-run equilibrium.

4.2 Exchange-rate dynamics

The monetary-approach model assumed instantaneous adjustment in all markets. An important modification was set forth by Dornbusch (1976). He assumed that asset markets adjust instantaneously, whereas prices in goods markets adjust more slowly. The resulting exchange-rate-dynamics model retains all the long-run-equilibrium, or steady-state, properties of the monetary approach. In the short run, however, the real exchange rate and the interest rate can diverge from their long-run levels, so that monetary policy can have effects on real variables in the system.

Exchange-rate dynamics, or "overshooting," can occur in any model in which some markets do not adjust instantaneously. When they do not, exchange-rate overshooting may accompany a perfectly foreseen adjustment process when goods prices adjust only slowly. That is, in response to a shock to the system (e.g., an increase in the money supply), the exchange rate will initially alter proportionately more than in the long run, so that its adjustment path to the new long-run equilibrium is opposite in direction from the initial impulse. An increase in the money supply, for example, leads to a proportionately larger once-and-for-all depreciation of the exchange rate, to be followed by exchange-rate appreciation throughout the rest of the adjustment process. Because, during the adjustment process, domestic prices are increasing while the exchange rate is appreciating, PPP does not hold except at long-run equilibrium.

Essentially, the domestic rate of interest always equals the world rate of interest plus the expected rate of increase in the domestic price of foreign currency, whereas the rate of increase in the exchange rate is a function of the divergence between the spot rate and the long-run rate. Given a log-linear demand for real money balances as a function of the domestic interest rate and real income, the time path of the domestic price level (as a function of the divergence between the spot and the long-run equilibrium level) and the time path of the exchange rate are linked through the relation

$$e = \bar{e} - (1/\lambda\phi)(p - \bar{p}) \qquad (4.14)$$

where e is the price of foreign exchange, λ and ϕ are the interest and income elasticities of demand for real balances (defined so that signs are positive), and bars over variables indicate long-run steady-state values. As can be seen, the price of foreign exchange is above its long-run level whenever the price level is below its long-run equilibrium level. When the price level is below its long-run level, so is nominal income (given constancy of real income), and hence so is the nominal demand for money at a given interest rate. Thus, the interest rate must be below its long-run value in order for the money supply to be willingly held. Therefore, on the adjustment path (with the rest of the world's price level constant), a rising domestic price level is accompanied by a rising interest rate, and therefore an appreciating exchange rate, even though PPP holds in the long run. Stated in another way, if the exchange rate did not initially overshoot, interest parity could not obtain along the adjustment path, and there would be a profitable arbitrage opportunity.

The nature of the adjustment process can most readily be understood with the use of Figure 4.1. The Q^0Q^0 line represents initial combinations of exchange rates and price levels that instantaneously clear the asset market for a given world interest rate and domestic money supply. It slopes downward via the relationship given in equation (4.14). The $\dot{p}_0 = 0$ line represents points at which the domestic-goods market clears associated with the same initial condition. Points below the $\dot{p} = 0$ line

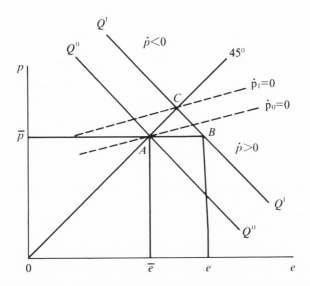

Figure 4.1. Exchange-rate overshooting.

represent points of excess demand for domestic goods, as the relative price of those goods (that price being p/e) is low (and the interest rate is also low), whereas points above the line represent excess supply. Because adjustment in the goods market is not instantaneous, the economy can in the short run be off the $\dot{p} = 0$ line but not off the QQ line.[36]

Consider, then, an (unanticipated) increase in the domestic money stock. That shifts the QQ line proportionally outward to Q^1Q^1 as higher prices at a depreciated exchange rate are required to clear the asset market. By homogeneity of the system, the $\dot{p} = 0$ line shifts up proportionally to the $\dot{p}_1$ line. The economy initially moves from the initial long-run-equilibrium

[36] The $\dot{p} = 0$ line is less steeply sloped than the 45-degree line, because given a constant money supply, an increase in domestic prices affects aggregate demand for domestic goods both by lowering the relative price of foreign goods and by raising the domestic interest rate.

point, A, to a new short-run-equilibrium point, B, on the new Q^1Q^1 line. At B, domestic prices are rising ($\dot{p} > 0$). This, in turn, leads to appreciation of the exchange rate (as the higher price level induces increased holdings of nominal money balances). The process continues until point C is reached, which is the new long-run-equilibrium combination of the price level and the exchange rate. As can be seen, the real exchange rate is unaltered in the long run. The system has all the normal homogeneity properties. In the short run, however, the initial depreciation of the exchange rate is greater than the long-run depreciation, so that the exchange rate appreciates on the path to the new long-run equilibrium.

The result comes about, of course, because of the assumption that asset markets clear instantaneously, whereas goods markets do not. Asset markets must bear the entire initial impact burden of adjustment, and this can occur only when the exchange rate overshoots; thereafter, expected currency appreciation offsets the interest-rate differential on the path to steady-state adjustment.

Overshooting will be less, the higher the interest response of money demand and the greater the expectations coefficient associated with divergences between spot and long-run exchange rates. The basic Dornbusch model is presented in the context of a constant domestic output level, but Dornbusch extended it to the case in which income is variable. The extent of overshooting is damped by income responses to changes in aggregate demand, and the phenomenon may in fact disappear entirely.

The overshooting result is consistent with perfect foresight. Initial shocks are unanticipated. Once they occur, however, overshooting clears the way for a time path of the domestic interest rate (given the world rate) and the exchange rate that is consistent with perfect foresight on the part of market participants. Indeed, given that an unanticipated increase in the domestic money supply would (temporarily) lower the domestic interest rate, expectations of currency appreciation are necessary in order to induce individuals to continue to hold domestic securities and money.

Recently, Frenkel and Rodriguez (1981) extended the Dornbusch analysis by considering the case in which there is finite speed of adjustment in asset markets as well as in goods markets. They showed that exchange-rate overshooting takes place with a sufficiently high degree of capital mobility; but with capital immobility, undershooting will result. This follows because with sufficient capital immobility, the interest rate is not so closely tied to the world rate plus the expected rate of currency appreciation. In their model, as in that of Dornbusch, it is the presence of a rigid nominal price in the short run that generates overshooting.

4.3 The portfolio approach

The monetary approach to exchange-rate determination and the balance of payments, although essentially a stock-flow approach, concentrates on domestic residents' demand for holding domestic money. By assuming perfect substitution between domestic and foreign bonds, the focus is on the single remaining asset.

By contrast, all variants of the portfolio approach emphasize some aspects of individuals' choices between holding domestic and foreign-currency-denominated assets. The models are differentiated chiefly in their assumptions about what individuals can and cannot hold and about the degree of substitutability between assets. Some assume that domestic residents hold only domestic money but may hold domestic and foreign bonds. Others assume that portfolio balance among various currencies may occur. Likewise, some models involve the small-country assumption, thereby implicitly examining portfolio choices within a framework in which foreign bonds and foreign money can be lumped via the composite-commodity theorem.

In the following sections we shall consider three topics. First, in Section 4.3.1 the basic Mundell-Fleming model is set forth. That model is appropriately regarded as the intellectual antecedent to the portfolio approach. Then, in Section 4.3.2 the elements of any portfolio-balance model of exchange-rate determination are outlined. In Section 4.3.3, currency-substitution models are examined.

4.3.1 *The Mundell-Fleming model*

Ironically, the line of thought that led to the 1974 monetary-approach model was actually closer intellectually to asset models than it was to the monetary approach to the balance of payments.[37] As already mentioned, Meade had in the 1950s focused on the possibility of incompatibility between the goals of external and internal balance. Motivated largely by the Canadian experience, Polak (1977), Fleming (1962), Mundell (1963), and others developed a Keynesian-type model in which the net current-account balance is a function of real income and the exchange rate (assuming Keynesian underemployment at a constant domestic price level), whereas the net capital-account balance is a function of the differential in interest rates between the home country and the rest of the world.[38] Real income, in turn, is a function of monetary and fiscal policy, increasing (via the multiplier) with increases in government expenditures and decreasing with the interest rate.

The point of the model was to demonstrate that the Meade conflict under fixed exchange rates need not exist with capital mobility. With two instruments – monetary policy and fiscal policy – and two targets – the balance of payments (not the current-account balance) and the level of real income – an appropriate combination of monetary and fiscal instruments

[37] Mundell (1963), Fleming (1962), and other writers on the "assignment problem" treated perfectly mobile capital as a special case and thus posited that capital flows would increase with increases in interest differentials.

[38] Conceptually, there are difficulties with treating the flow of asset accumulation as a function of the interest rate or interest-rate differentials. Presumably, the desired level of asset holdings is a stock, and one would have to explain why stock adjustment to the desired level was not instantaneous. It is in remedying this defect that portfolio models go beyond the Mundell-Fleming model.

could achieve both targets. Apparently, therefore, the potential conflicts between external balance and internal balance under fixed exchange rates might be resolved if appropriate assignments of instruments to targets were made.[39]

Formally, the model is elementary. For simplicity, the small-country case is set forth here, although extension to a two-country world is straightforward. The small-country assumption permits taking the world interest rate and prices as given. Hence,

$$\text{NCA} = X(Y, E) - M(Y, E)$$
$$\frac{\partial X}{\partial Y} < 0; \quad \frac{\partial X}{\partial E} > 0; \quad \frac{\partial M}{\partial Y} > 0; \quad \frac{\partial M}{\partial E} < 0 \quad (4.15)$$

$$I = I(i); \quad \frac{\partial I}{\partial i} > 0 \quad (4.16)$$

$$B \equiv \text{NCA} + I \quad (4.17)$$

$$Y = Y(G, i, E); \quad \frac{\partial Y}{\partial G} > 0; \quad \frac{\partial Y}{\partial i} < 0; \quad \frac{\partial Y}{\partial E} > 0 \quad (4.18)$$

where NCA is the net current-account balance and X is exports (a function of Y, nominal income, and E, the price of foreign exchange), with the partial derivatives as indicated. The fact that no domestic price level appears in the model reflects the implicit assumption of an underemployment equilibrium of the type in which an increase in aggregate demand can increase real income without any accompanying increase in domestic prices.[40] I is the net capital inflow to the country (which might be positive or negative); B is then the balance of payments, G is government expenditures (or tax receipts, with opposite signs on all derivatives), and i is the rate of interest. Equation (4.18) is a reduced form, because real income increases with aggregate

[39] A major thrust was to contrast the effects of monetary and fiscal policy under fixed and flexible exchange rates. That subject is deferred to Chapter 6.

[40] To permit some price increase in conjunction with higher levels of real income does not alter the results, but real income must respond to increases in aggregate demand. See Krueger(1965) for one such extension.

demand, which is positively related to government expenditures and the exchange rate and negatively related to the interest rate.

Differentiating totally with respect to the exogenous variables, G and i, and holding the exchange rate constant, yields

$$dY = \frac{\partial Y}{\partial G} dG + \frac{\partial Y}{\partial i} di \qquad (4.19)$$

$$dB = \left(\overset{-}{\frac{\partial X}{\partial Y}} - \overset{+}{\frac{\partial M}{\partial Y}}\right)\left(\frac{\partial Y}{\partial G} dG + \overset{-}{\frac{\partial Y}{\partial i}} di\right) + \overset{+}{\frac{\partial I}{\partial i}} di \qquad (4.20)$$

As can be seen, any combination of income and balance-of-payments targets may be compatible. For a given real income, the balance of payments can always be improved by raising both the interest rate and the level of government expenditures (or lowering taxes). For a given balance of payments, real income can always be increased by raising both.

This can be seen graphically in Figure 4.2. The line Y_0 represents combinations of interest rates and fiscal policies that will yield a given real income, whereas B_0 represents those combinations resulting in a particular balance-of-payments position, B_0. Y_0 slopes upward because more government expenditures are required to maintain a given level of real income the higher the interest rate. B_0 slopes upward because a higher real income can be offset only by a higher interest rate. If capital flows were perfectly elastic with respect to the interest rate, B_0 would be parallel to the horizontal axis, because the deterioration in the current-account balance with rising incomes would be offset by increased capital flows.[41] The composition of the balance of payments along the B_0 line is shifting: As one moves northeast, the current-account deficit is increasing (as real income rises) and the net capital inflow (outflow) is increasing (decreasing).

---

[41] Strictly speaking, the balance of payments is indeterminate if the supply of foreign capital is perfectly elastic at the prevailing interest rate.

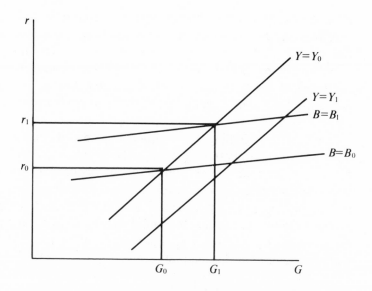

Figure 4.2. External balance and internal balance.

If the authorities were satisfied with the prevailing balance of payments, but wished to attain a higher real income, the Mundell-Fleming model would imply that they should shift the mix of monetary policy and fiscal policy. In Figure 4.2, a target income level of Y_1 could be achieved from an initial level Y_0 by shifting the governmental expenditure level from G_0 to G_1, while tightening monetary policy so that the domestic interest rate would rise from r_0 to r_1. Similar reasoning would apply to improving the balance-of-payments position (decreasing the reserve outflow or increasing the inflow) going from B_0 to B_1 (not drawn).

The model has several shortcomings. First, it neglects the impact of increasing short-term indebtedness (as a consequence of borrowing abroad with tighter monetary policy) on the future balance of payments. Obviously, should a country continue to incur current-account deficits indefinitely, the mounting foreign debt incurred to cover them would have increasing debt servicing costs associated with it over time. It therefore must be the case that the Mundell-Fleming analysis is short run in scope. Second, the treatment of capital flows is unsatisfactory for reasons already mentioned: All modern asset theory suggests that capital flows are consequences of adaptations to desired stock positions. This leads directly to the portfolio models to be discussed later.

The Mundell-Fleming contribution was to call economists' attention to the important fact that the balance of payments consists of both current-account and capital-account transactions. Any satisfactory analysis of exchange-rate determination and of the balance of payments must take capital flows into account. In this sense, the Mundell-Fleming analysis was the precursor to the monetary approach as well as to all other models discussed in this chapter.

4.3.2 *The basic portfolio–balance model*

It appears that several lines of thought independently originated the portfolio-balance approach.[42] McKinnon (1969) and McKinnon and Oates (1966) early pointed out the deficiencies of treating capital flows as a function of the interest rate in the Mundell-Fleming model. Branson (1975) modeled the portfolio approach at a fairly early stage, basing his model on Tobin's monetary models.[43] More recent studies have been numerous: Allen (1973), Boyer (1977), Branson (1977), Branson, Halttunen, and Masson (1977), Dornbusch (1975a), and Allen and Kenen (1976). As already mentioned, Frenkel and Rodriguez (1975) concentrated on desired net asset accumulation as the determinant of the current-account balance, within the context of the monetary approach, thus providing a bridge between the 1974 model and later work.

---

[42] For a careful, systematic exposition of the portfolio-balance model, see Allen and Kenen (1980).

[43] Some publication dates are misleading. The McKinnon (1969) paper was presented at a conference in 1966, and Branson's 1975 paper was a conference paper in 1974.

Central to all portfolio models is the notion that individuals allocate their wealth, which is fixed at a point in time, among alternative assets, including, most generally, domestic and foreign money and domestic and foreign securities. In a simple one-country model, in which individuals cannot hold foreign currency, the basic equations are

$$M = \alpha(i, i^*)W \qquad (4.21)$$
$$B = \beta(i, i^*)W \qquad (4.22)$$
$$EF = \gamma(i, i^*)W \qquad (4.23)$$
$$W = M + B + EF \qquad (4.24)$$

where M is domestic money, B is the supply of domestic assets, F is the net holdings of foreign assets, E is the price of foreign exchange, i is the nominal interest rate, and W is initial wealth. Obviously, from (4.24), the sum of α, β, and γ must be unity, so that (4.21), (4.22), and (4.23) are not independent. Of course, F can be either positive or negative, depending on whether a country is a net creditor or debtor.

It is usually assumed that the demand for domestic money decreases with increases in either the domestic or the foreign interest rate, whereas the demand for domestic bonds increases with the domestic interest rate and falls with the foreign interest rate.[44] These assumptions are sufficient to ensure that the demand for foreign bonds increases with the foreign interest rate and with decreases in the domestic interest rate.

In the form set forth in equations (4.21) through (4.24), the ratios of wealth held in the three asset types are independent of exchange-rate expectations. For later purposes, however, it is worthwhile observing that, given the wealth definition (4.24), a change in the exchange rate, E, will lead to a change in total wealth and also to an altered demand for foreign securities, F. The role of the exchange rate is one of balancing asset demands and supplies, given domestic money supplies and assets.

[44] It may be noted that the demand-for-money function no longer has income as a direct argument. Desired wealth, however, is a function of income.

The equilibrium condition for the market for foreign assets is

$$EF = (1 - \alpha - \beta)W = g(i, i^*)W \qquad (4.25)$$

This condition can be rewritten as

$$E = g(i, i^*) \frac{W}{F} \qquad (4.26)$$

This is one of several equivalent ways of stating that the exchange rate is the price at which individuals willingly hold the stocks of domestic and foreign assets. It is assumed that domestic and foreign interest rates are determined by conditions of asset-market equilibrium. Focus is on the role of the exchange rate in bringing about portfolio balance; any change in the exchange rate brings about capital gains and capital losses.

Consider, for example, an exogenous decrease in the demand for imports. This would instantaneously lead to an increment in total wealth, because the current account would go into surplus. According to relations (4.21) through (4.26), domestic residents would wish to hold more domestic securities and fewer foreign securities.[45] In an effort to restore desired portfolio balance, domestic residents would wish to sell some of their holdings of foreign securities. This would constitute an excess supply of foreign currency, and hence the exchange rate would tend to appreciate. Thus, a current-account surplus is seen to affect the exchange rate via its effect on asset holdings and the instantaneous restoration of portfolio balances.

What is emphasized in this line of reasoning is the response of individuals to changes in their holdings of wealth. The exchange rate adjusts to induce individuals willingly to hold actual stocks of domestic and foreign assets. The view is that it is the capital account (not the current account) that is rapidly responsive to exchange-rate changes, and, alternatively, the

---

[45] The exposition assumes that F is positive. The argument is symmetric if F is negative.

exchange rate plays a major role in permitting individuals to hold their desired portfolios.

Starting from an initial equilibrium in the portfolio-balance model, one can investigate the impact of changes in domestic money, foreign interest rates, or net external assets. Consider first an increase in the foreign interest rate from an initial situation of portfolio balance under floating exchange rates. Such an increase raises the desired fraction of wealth held in foreign assets; this shifts outward the demand for foreign exchange, which in turn leads to currency depreciation (thereby partially satisfying the increased demand for foreign assets).

Next, consider an increase in the domestic money stock. It generates an excess demand for domestic and foreign securities and an excess supply of money. The equilibrium exchange rate depreciates in response to the capital outflow. We thus have the predictions of the monetary approach to the balance of payments as a special case of the portfolio-balance model.[46]

Finally, under the homogeneity assumptions built into equations (4.21) through (4.24), a proportionate increase in domestic securities and money stock results in a proportionate increase in the price of foreign exchange. Thus, under floating exchange rates, an inflation process is neutral, just as it is under the monetary approach, although nominal interest rates are affected.

As set forth here, the portfolio-balance model is "partial" in several senses. First, it abstracts from determinants of real income and real domestic wealth and interactions between them. Second, the model is unsatisfactory in that there is no treatment at all of flows of goods and services. Third (related to the second factor in ways that will become evident in Chapter

---

[46] Without further assumptions, the sign of the partial derivative of the exchange rate with respect to changes in the stock of domestic securities is ambiguous. There is a sense in which this consideration highlights one of the "partial" aspects of the portfolio-balance approach: If the supply of domestic securities increases as an offset to increases in real wealth, the effect may conceivably be quite different than if, say, government debt is created.

5), there is no role for expectations in the portfolio-balance model described by equations (4.21) through (4.26). Finally, but far less important, is the consideration that the model as presented pertains only to one country.

The appeal of the portfolio-balance approach lies in several of its features. First, as will be seen in Chapter 5, it can more readily be adapted to incorporate current-account phenomena and expectations than can the monetary approach. Second, by allowing for imperfect substitutability between assets, the port-folio-balance model is more general than the monetary approach. Finally, the fact that some of the assumptions under-pinning the monetary approach are violated by empirical reality renders the portfolio-balance model more tempting in that it conforms somewhat more closely to at least one important aspect of reality.

What seems empirically valid, at least for some currencies (and this is the major insight of the portfolio approach), is that the existing stocks of domestic and foreign securities must be willingly held; their volume far outweighs the current account at any given moment. Hence, the exchange rate in the short run reflects conditions of equilibrium in the asset market.

4.3.3 *Currency-substitution models*

Both the portfolio-balance and monetary approaches essentially assume that the alternative to holding domestic money or assets is either holding foreign assets or increasing current-account spending. As such, they implicitly or explicitly assume that domestic residents do not hold foreign currency (or that they hold it in amounts that are invariant with respect to interest-rate differentials, the spot–forward exchange-rate rela-tionship, deviations from PPP, and so on).

A number of related models have instead focused on individ-uals' portfolio choices in their holdings of monies of different denominations. In formal structure, the similarity to the port-folio-balance models is striking. In a sense, one can argue that they really represent portfolio-balance models in which the interest rate on assets is zero. In economic interpretation, however, there are some points of substance that differ from the portfolio-balance approach.

The essential notion behind all the currency-substitution models is that individuals' demand for money is defined not for domestic currency but for a group of currencies. As such, individuals' demand for domestic currency may or may not be a well-defined and stable function. This point, of course, goes to the core of monetary theory and monetary policy, as well as to the question of the degree to which the domestic monetary authority can affect in a meaningful way the quantity of money.

There are two types of currency-substitution models. There are some that interpret any current-account surpluses or deficits as reflecting excess demand or supply of domestic currency relative to foreign currency. These models are similar to models of the monetary approach to the balance of payments (the 1974 model, discussed earlier) in that the capital account and capital markets are largely neglected. The models of Barro (1978) and Calvo and Rodriguez (1977) are of this type and are relatively straightforward to expound. The second class of currency-substitution models have a different focus: They view the money supply as being a worldwide phenomenon within the context of a highly integrated world capital market. To distinguish these two very different approaches, the Barro-Calvo-Rodriguez approach is termed monetary currency substitution; those taking the second approach are termed global currency-substitution models.

Turning first to the monetary currency-substitution models, the key notion is that the only asset, money, has two components. Following Calvo and Rodriguez,[47]

$$a = m + eD \qquad (4.27)$$

---

[47] Barro's model is similar, although he emphasized the importance of the expected exchange rate and its simultaneous determination with the spot rate. In that regard, his model is close to the rational-expectations models discussed in Chapter 5.

where a is the real value of assets in terms of home goods, m is the real stock of money in terms of home goods (i.e., $m = M/p_h$, where M is the nominal stock of domestic currency and p_h is the price of home goods), $e = E/p_h$ is the real exchange rate (with E the nominal exchange rate), and D is the domestically held and owned stock of foreign currency. It is assumed that foreigners do not hold domestic currency. Note that D might almost as readily be interpreted as foreign bonds, except that it is assumed non-interest-bearing.[48]

The crucial point is that the real rate of return on holding domestic money is minus the rate of domestic inflation, because the nominal rate of return is zero. The real rate on holding foreign currency is the rate of depreciation of the exchange rate minus the rate of domestic inflation (assuming stable prices abroad for the sake of exposition).

With normal assumptions about real output and consumption (of home and traded goods) responses to relative prices, it is easily shown that, at any point in time, real assets are a decreasing function of the real exchange rate, whereas the change in holdings of foreign currency is an increasing function of the real exchange rate.

Currency substitution is built into the model by assuming that the desired ratio of domestic to foreign currency holdings is a function of the expected difference in rates of return, which is equal to the actual rate of change in the exchange rate, given perfect foresight. Thus,

$$dE/E = L(m/eD) \qquad (4.28)$$

Because the rate of accumulation of foreign currency is a function of the real exchange rate, whereas the rate of change in the nominal exchange rate depends on the real exchange rate and the stock of foreign currency (for any given domestic real

---

[48] There is an underlying question as to why any money (rather than bonds) is held at all. Alternative answers include transactions costs, the Clower liquidity constraint (see Section 5.3), and overlapping generations, where money is the only store of value.

money supply), there exists a steady-state solution for the real exchange rate and real stocks of each currency for any given rate of domestic monetary growth. One can examine the changes in the solution with respect to disturbances in the system, and overshooting occurs much as in the Dornbusch model.[49] In the Calvo-Rodriguez model, it is the slowness of portfolio adjustment that gives rise to the phenomenon. For example, a higher rate of monetary expansion leads to an immediate jump in the exchange rate, a jump of smaller proportions in the price of home goods, and higher steady-state holdings of foreign exchange. Faster monetary growth implies faster exchange-rate depreciation, which, with rational expectations, implies that individuals will shift their portfolio composition toward foreign currency. Because adjustment is not instantaneous (and can be achieved only through current-account surpluses), depreciation of the currency initially lowers real wealth, and the demand for nontradables thereby shifts downward. The relative price of nontradables must therefore fall (the real exchange rate must depreciate). As current-account surpluses gradually increase real wealth, the real exchange rate appreciates toward its long-run value.[50]

Several things are of interest in this model. First, its overshooting arises because asset adjustments are slow, whereas in the Dornbusch model it is because goods prices adjust slowly. Second, it shares with many other models the feature that the current-account balance varies in the short run in response to changes in the real exchange rate, but only as part of a dynamic process in which both alter over time to a new equilibrium with

---

[49] In the Dornbusch model, overshooting occurs as the short-run change exceeds the long-run equilibrium change. In the Calvo-Rodriguez model, overshooting occurs because the movement of the nominal rate exceeds what would keep the real rate constant at its long-run-equilibrium level.

[50] In the Calvo-Rodriguez model, a once-and-for-all unanticipated increase in the money supply is neutral because the expected rate of inflation, and hence the desired holding of foreign currency, is unaffected.

a zero current-account balance. Third, Frenkel and Rodriguez (1981) interpreted the overshooting result in an interesting way. They argued the following:

> Since the foreign currency price of traded goods is assumed to be given, the accumulation of foreign currency is equivalent to an accumulation of claims on stocks of traded goods. With this perspective the currency substitution model can be specified in terms of choice and substitution between domestic money and traded goods. It is intuitively clear therefore that following the rise in the rate of monetary expansion asset holders wish to hedge against the expected inflation by shifting the composition of portfolios toward the inflation hedge (traded goods), a shift which results, in the short run, in a rise in the relative price of traded goods [p. 21].

They proceeded to show that if nontraded goods were the inflation hedge within the same model, the impact effect of an increase in the expected rate of inflation would be exchange-rate undershooting.

Whereas the monetary currency-substitution models focus on the effects of changes in the exchange rate on holdings of foreign currency (and vice versa) from the viewpoint a single currency, the global currency-substitution models essentially focus on the dependency between monies. The points at issue are best understood by considering the extreme case in which individuals hold whatever money is cheapest to hold. Obviously, the cheapest money to hold is the one with the lowest rate of inflation. Hence, the monies that are willingly held in portfolios must all have the same expected rate of inflation.

Wallace (1979) has perhaps been the foremost advocate of this view. Monies of different countries are seen as perfect substitutes, and therefore the exchange rate for any particular pair of currencies is indeterminate. This follows in the Wallace model because it is assumed that there is something like a global Cambridge equation determining the world price level: A different exchange rate for a particular currency affects the world price level via its impact on the world money supply.

This fundamental indeterminacy provides a reason why exchange rates are highly volatile, as well as a reason why the government should fix the exchange rate. For individuals concerned about possible inconsistencies in a world with diverging rates of inflation, Wallace would answer that individuals will eliminate the more rapidly inflating currencies from their portfolios.

Most models, however, focus on currency substitution that is less than perfect.[51] In these models, individuals hold both currencies as money for transactions and other purposes. The desired composition of currency holdings (in each country and in a two-country world) is a function of the ratio of interest rates: The higher the home country's interest rate, the higher the fraction of money that will be held in the foreign currency (because opportunity costs of holding it are lower). This, of course, assumes that individuals in both countries can and do hold securities nominally denominated in both currencies in an integrated (but less than perfectly so) capital market.

The essential feature of the global currency-substitution model can best be seen by considering the comparative statics of an increase in the supply of the home currency. Such a one-shot increase leads to an increase in home prices (thus somewhat offsetting the initial real increase in cash balances) and a decrease in the home interest rate. This makes holding home currency more attractive to both domestic residents and foreigners. As foreigners (and domestic residents) switch from holding their currency to holding foreign currency, prices in the foreign country also rise.[52]

Hence, because of currency substitution, the once-and-for-all

---

[51] An early currency-substitution model was that of Girton and Roper, which was available in mimeograph form, dated 1976, for a long time prior to its publication in 1981.

[52] Note that this follows from an implicit assumption that there is a home good in each country, not from the law of one price.

increase in money stock in the home country is equivalent to an increase in the world money supply. Inflation is transmitted through currency substitution: The greater the substitutability of currencies, the greater the degree of transmission.

Bilson (1979) characterized the global currency-substitution models as being distinguishable from others by their assumption that the real value of any currency in a portfolio is measured by its purchasing power over a standard bundle of (international) traded goods: "The fundamental determinants of the exchange rate are assumed to be the relative supplies of the two currencies and the relative holding cost as measured by the interest rate differential" (Bilson, 1979, p. 211). It will be seen later that these models are consistent with rational-expectations models and that the question is really an empirical one: whether currencies are highly substitutable (whether held for transactions or store-of-value purposes) or whether, instead, it is unanticipated news and its high variance (the asset approach of most of this chapter) or current-account/capital-account interactions (the subject of Chapter 5) that lead to exchange-rate changes.

4.4 Expectations and the exchange rate

The capital-account models discussed in Sections 4.2, 4.3.2, and 4.3.3 all focus to some degree on expectations and on whether or not a speculator, knowing the underlying structure of the model, could make abnormal profits in an economy so structured. Clearly, the role of expectations has assumed center stage in the theory of exchange-rate determination, and it is appropriate to end this chapter with a brief survey of the literature that has been important in contributing to our understanding of the role of expectations.

Argy and Porter (1972), Black (1973), Niehans (1977), and Mussa (1976) were among those who highlighted the role of expectations in the context of monetary, or capital-account-oriented, approaches to the determination of exchange rates. Kouri's analysis (1976) is perhaps most useful in illuminating the role of expectations. He developed a model of exchange-rate determination in the context of (1) traded goods only, so that the exchange rate is also the domestic price level, (2) full employment, so that real income is exogenous, and (3) only domestic residents hold domestic money. Assuming that domestic absorption is a function of government expenditures and domestic consumption (a function of disposable income and real wealth, which includes domestic money deflated by the price level – or exchange rate – and foreign assets that do not bear interest), the trade balance is positive when income is in excess of absorption. Stated another way, the trade balance is positive when individuals are increasing their holdings of foreign assets and negative when they are reducing them. In conformity with most capital-account models, Kouri's model distinguishes momentary equilibrium from steady-state equilibrium,[53] and one can alternatively state that short-run "equilibrium in the asset markets determines the exchange rate," or that "the exchange rate is determined to *equilibrate the demand for foreign assets with the existing stock of foreign assets.*"[54] The stationary state occurs when wealth holdings are constant over time, and the exchange-rate path corresponds to the inflation differential with no net change in foreign wealth.[55]

Kouri investigated the dynamic stability of the adjustment process under alternative assumptions. He found, not surprisingly, that in a static expectations model there would be unexploited profit opportunities for speculators.

In the case of myopic perfect foresight (in which case the

---

[53] Kouri's article forcefully made the point that the balance-of-payments accounts are an ex-post identity and that any identification of them with the ex-ante demand for asset acquisition (given the assumption of instantaneous adjustments of portfolios to desired levels) must assume perfect foresight.

[54] Kouri (1976, p. 284). Kouri noted that the strong separation in markets holds because of his assumption of no home goods. See Section 5.1 for a model in which current and capital accounts interact.

[55] In most dynamic models with nonzero rates of inflation, depreciation in the steady-state exchange rate refers to a shift in the entire time path of the exchange rate.

expected rate of depreciation equals the expected rate of domestic inflation, which in turn equals the current realized rate), there exists a time path of the exchange rate and foreign assets in which all markets are in equilibrium for any initial exchange rate. In this sense, the exchange rate is indeterminate. Of all possible paths, there is only one along which the economy can converge to a stationary state. Others diverge, and either hyperinflation or hyperdeflation eventually results. As Kouri pointed out, with long-run perfect foresight, speculators will anticipate that hyperdeflation cannot continue once foreign assets are drawn down to zero and hence prevent hyperdeflation from being realized. In the case of hyperinflation, speculators with perfect foresight would eliminate all domestic currency immediately unless there were some minimal level of real balances necessary to carry out transactions. In that case, the end of hyperinflation might again be anticipated, and rational speculation would rule it out. When these cases are eliminated, it turns out that an exchange rate based on PPP is the only one consistent with expectations formations based on the assumptions of the model – the rational-expectations path.

Kouri's main contribution was to show how sensitive the dynamic stability of the exchange-rate path and the adjustment process was to the assumptions made about expectations formation. Barro and Bilson have also constructed rational-expectations models in which exchange-rate expectations are based on the model itself. Bilson's model focuses on combining the monetary approach with "efficient-markets" hypotheses. His building blocks are those discussed in Section 4.1.4: purchasing power parity; interest-rate parity (i.e., the equalization of real rates of return); the Fisher condition that the nominal rate of interest equals the real rate plus the expected rate of inflation; and the rational-expectations hypothesis, that market price expectations will be formed based on the predictions of the model itself.

Within the model, present and expected future values of the money supply and the level of real income (itself determined by unanticipated changes in the money supply) determine present and future values of the price level. This, using the Fisher condition, gives the expected rate of inflation and the term structure of nominal interest rates. From those rates and the PPP condition, the spot and forward exchange rates are determined. Of particular interest is that the forward exchange rate is an unbiased, or efficient, estimate of the future spot exchange rate.

Within the efficient-markets model, all arbitrage opportunities for profit are exhausted, while simultaneously speculators' anticipations are rational. Therefore, all that remains to affect the behavior of the exchange rate is unanticipated changes in variables. If, for example, the expected rate of increase in the money supply increases, the model predicts a large response in the exchange rate (and, indeed, there may be overshooting as in other models). If, on the other hand, an unexpectedly large increase in the money supply in this period leads to expectations of a smaller than average increase next period, exchange-rate markets may be unaffected.

A key characteristic of all the expectations models of this type is that any change in expectations now affects both the spot and forward exchange rates and the structure of interest rates now.[56] If, for example, there were a "surprise announcement" today that starting in six months the rate of monetary expansion would accelerate, the spot and forward rates would both depreciate today, and interest rates would adjust to the revised expectations. There is no presumption that when the rate of monetary expansion in fact increases six months hence there will be any impact on the path of the spot or forward exchange rate at that time.

Bilson's analysis puts into clear focus the role of expectations about the money-supply process. The exchange rate will move sharply with changes in the money supply if the process is, as he terms it, "unstable" – that is, unanticipated changes lead to expectations of further changes in the same direction. If, on the

---

[56] See Wilson (1979).

other hand, expectations are "stable," anticipating reversal of current surprises, the exchange rate will move little with unanticipated changes. As Bilson pointed out, there is an important difference between an unstable process (in which changes lead to expectations of further change in the same direction) and an unpredictable process (which simply implies a large variance and prediction error).

Most of the models discussed in Chapter 5 have rational expectations built into them. Although expectations are not always central to the focus of analysis, the volatility that arises from efficient-markets hypotheses in the context of expectations being formed from the underlying model is a forecast that emerges from all of them.

4.5 Conclusions

All the models discussed in this chapter have assigned a central role to one or more features of a stock adjustment and the capital account in exchange-rate determination or balance-of-payments adjustment. It was probably the implicit assumption of perfect substitutability of foreign and domestic bonds in the Mundell-Fleming model that led to the original focus on the monetary approach to the balance of payments and exchange-rate determination. Such an initial emphasis was replaced with a shift in attention to stock-flow adjustments, and that is probably the central, lasting contribution of the monetary approach as it was conceived in the early 1970s.

By contrast, currency-substitution models and portfolio-balance models both assume that individuals can hold more than one type of asset and that there is generally less than perfect substitutability between them. As such, interdependencies and linkages among asset markets in different countries become a focal point of attention. Expectations are important in all of these models, as focus shifts to the "news" that leads to changes in asset prices in efficient markets.

Even these models, as presented here, have certain shortcomings. In particular, the price of assets presumably reflects the capitalized value of an income stream; to treat trade in assets without regard to current-account transactions and to disregard the impact of the exchange rate on current-account transactions seems unsatisfactory. We therefore turn to models that attempt to link current-account and capital-account transactions.

5

Interactions between current account and capital account

As seen earlier, models of exchange-rate determination and the balance of payments focused largely on the current account in the 1960s and on the capital account in the early and middle 1970s. Although incorporation of the role of asset markets was obviously a major step forward in the analysis of exchange-rate determination, there were grounds for dissatisfaction. Perhaps because of earlier emphasis, and perhaps for other reasons, many economists felt that total neglect of the exchange rate's impact on trade in goods and services missed something important. Assets are a stock, and a flow (i.e., current-account imbalance) is necessary to acquire or dispose of them. Neglect of the current-account, or flow, relation seemed unwarranted on this ground.

There was finally the fact that developments in the latter part of the 1970s did not seem to accord with the asset-market-only story, in at least two important regards. Countries in current-account surplus tended to have appreciating exchange rates, whereas those in current-account deficit more often experienced depreciating exchange rates, an observation that could not be forecast from asset models. Likewise, deviations from PPP seemed to many observers to be larger than could be explained only by "news," and a search began for models of exchange-rate determination that might contain PPP and other variables as arguments. In this process, of course, the question immedi-

102

ately reemerges as to the role of the exchange rate as a real, or relative-price, variable.

Three interrelated analytical developments have brought the current account back into the focus of analysis in response to these concerns. First, recognition that changes in asset holdings can come about only through imbalances on current account has focused attention on the current-account surplus or deficit as inevitably being accompanied by asset accumulation or decumulation. Models differ as to whether asset motives prompt current-account imbalances or conversely, but all recognize that current-account surpluses and deficits affect the size of foreign-asset holdings. Second, rational-expectations models of exchange-rate determination have been developed that focus on particular aspects of links between current account and capital account, including (1) the recognition that the expected future current-account path implies an expectation of the future path of foreign-asset accumulation and consequently an expectation about future prices of those assets and (2) the identification of exchange-rate changes with terms-of-trade shifts in response to real disturbances. Finally, analysis of the current-account balance as an expression of savings behavior has focused attention on the intertemporal aspects of current-account/capital-account linkages and their role in exchange-rate determination.

Work on current-account/capital-account interactions is a very recent phenomenon, although earlier studies by Kouri (1976) and Niehans (1977) anticipated it. With very few exceptions, there has been no attempt to incorporate investment decisions into these models, so that capital stock is implicitly taken as given and the assets under discussion are financial assets. Because the current-account balance is, by definition, the ex-post difference between investment and saving, the exclusive focus on savings is unsatisfactory.[1]

---

[1] See Sachs (1981) for an attempt to integrate investment behavior into the analysis. He attempted to explore current-account swings in the 1970s by shifts in investment behavior in the face of stable saving behavior.

Of the contributions to be surveyed here, not all are in print, and none has been in print for even a year as of the time of writing (winter 1981). It is a reasonable hypothesis that the major developments of the next several years in understanding exchange-rate determination will lie in further exploration of the very complex links between current-account and capital-account transactions under alternative specifications of the menu of assets available to domestic residents and foreigners, the speed with which various markets clear, investment behavior, and other variables.

What seems fairly clear at this juncture is that there is an emerging view of exchange-rate determination as a function of financial asset-market variables in the short run and current-account variables in the long run.[2] Stylistically, the outline of the story is approximately the following. In the long run, there is a current-account balance compatible with domestic residents' time preferences relative to investment opportunities at the world rate of interest (which may be a function of the net asset position of the country). That determines the long-run real exchange rate (the price of tradables relative to home goods) on its time path. The real exchange rate could alter gradually over time because of different time preferences relative to the rest of the world as the net indebtedness position changed, or it could shift because of exogenous changes in time preference, wealth, or other variables, but its determinants are always long-run. Given the long-run real exchange rate as determined by the current account, at any point in time, the asset market determines the exchange rate. Existing stocks of foreign-denominated assets change their values in response to exchange-rate changes and influence wealth (as in the story in Chapter 4). Because the current-account imbalances then impact on wealth positions over time, the adjustment of wealth to changing current-

---

[2] The Allen-Kenen volume (1980) anticipates a great deal of the results of the interaction models and provides a systematic exposition of much of the analysis.

account balances is the mechanism through which the short run becomes the long run.

There are many pieces of the foregoing statement that have only begun to be sketched in, and mechanisms differ in different models. In this chapter, therefore, some of the models already developed will be surveyed. This chapter is perforce briefer and less complete than the rest of the volume, and the reader interested only in well-established "received doctrine" can skim over much of the detail here. The first section reviews work on the links between the current account and changing stocks of foreign assets. The second covers a rational-expectations model of the foreign-exchange market in the "elasticities" tradition. The third section then turns to models of intertemporal maximization and the role of exchange rates in affecting the maximization process.

5.1 **The current account and the demand for assets**

In an interesting and seminal study that has not yet been published, Kouri (1978) attempted to analyze the current-account/capital-account linkages in the context of a "dynamic, partial-equilibrium" model. His analysis focused on the determinants of the demand for, and supply of, foreign exchange in the foreign-exchange market.[3] He argued as follows:

> All economic transactions between countries or regions
> that belong to a different currency area must go
> through the foreign exchange market. Domestic resi-
> dents wishing to purchase goods and services or assets
> abroad must first acquire foreign currency . . . Going
> through the foreign exchange market would not be
> necessary if domestic money was acceptable as a
> means of payment abroad and foreign money as a

---

[3] The model is "partial equilibrium" in nature because only the foreign-exchange market is analyzed. Later it will be seen that the Dornbusch-Fischer results represent a general-equilibrium extension of much the same model.

means of payment at home. Since this is not the case,
planned domestic payments abroad translate to
demand for, and planned foreign payments at home to
supply of, foreign currency in the foreign exchange
market [p. 1].

He proceeded to develop a model in which the current-
account demands for and supplies of foreign exchange match
up with capital-account supplies and demands to equilibrate the
foreign-exchange market in the absence of intervention. The
exchange rate adjusts so as to equate the current-account surplus with the capital-account deficit (acquisition of foreign
assets), and vice versa.

It was seen in Chapter 4 that many asset models of exchange-
rate determination essentially posit that the fractions of wealth
held in domestic money, assets denominated in domestic currency, and assets denominated in foreign currency are functions
of such variables as nominal and real interest rates and differentials in them, expected rates of currency depreciation, and so
on. Given the parameters that determine those fractions, the
demand for foreign exchange on capital account has unit price
elasticity. This follows because the fraction of wealth to be held
in foreign-denominated assets is constant as a function of interest rates and other variables. For given holdings of foreign-
denominated assets, an increase in the price of foreign exchange
will induce domestic residents to sell foreign securities to reattain their desired portfolio balance and will induce foreigners to
buy more assets denominated in domestic currency to restore
their balance.

Simultaneously, on current account, the current-account balance is an increasing function of the price of foreign exchange
for the home country. In the foreign-exchange market, the
demand for foreign exchange consists of the sum of the current-
account demand and capital-account demand. A country in current-account surplus must experience a currency appreciation
to induce domestic residents to acquire additional foreign securities (equal in amount to the current-account surplus); a coun-

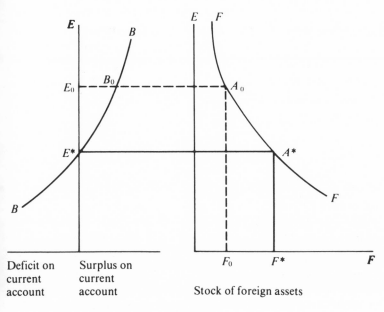

Figure 5.1. The Kouri diagram.

try in deficit must experience currency depreciation in order to induce sales of foreign-denominated securities and thus a capital-account surplus to offset the current-account deficit. This accounts for the stylized fact that countries in surplus on current account appreciate, and countries in deficit depreciate. Kouri termed the phenomenon the acceleration hypothesis.

The basic model is illustrated in Figure 5.1, on the special assumption that foreign residents do not hold domestic assets. Then, the short-run condition for equilibrium in the foreign-exchange market is that

$$F \cdot E = f(i, i^* + \pi, z)V \tag{5.1}$$

where F is the stock of foreign assets held by domestic residents, E is the spot price of foreign exchange, f is the fraction of wealth to be held in foreign assets, i and i^* are the nominal rates of return on domestic and foreign assets in their own currency, π is the expected rate of change in the domestic-currency price of foreign currency, and z is a vector of other determinants of international portfolio-balance considerations.

Thus, with an initial stock of assets of F_0 in Figure 5.1, the initial equilibrium is at exchange rate E_0, with a current-account surplus in the amount of B_0. The stock of foreign assets therefore changes according to

$$\dot{F} = B(E, y) \tag{5.2}$$

where y is a vector of the determinants of the current account, including domestic and foreign prices and real incomes.

As the stock of foreign assets increases, the currency appreciates, as the market moves to long-run equilibrium at A^*, with the exchange rate E^* and the stock of foreign assets F^*. Given that the current account is in surplus at higher prices of foreign exchange and that asset accumulation is consistent with equilibrium only with an appreciating exchange rate, the long-run-equilibrium exchange rate is unique and globally stable.

There are several intriguing features of the model. In response to a disturbance in the foreign-exchange market, the exchange rate at any moment in time is a weighted average of the long-run-equilibrium exchange rate (the rate at which the current account is in balance in the Kouri model) and the short-run-equilibrium rate (the rate that clears the asset market). Short-term factors are more important in influencing the rate at any point in time the smaller is the responsiveness of the current account to exchange-rate changes and the more important are trade flows relative to foreign-asset holdings.[4] Thus, if there were two countries subjected to disturbances of the same magnitude, the country with relatively larger trade flows contrasted

---

[4] Kouri derived these results in the context of stationary prices and constant real incomes in both countries. This again demonstrates the partial-equilibrium nature of the model. Even more important, perhaps, is the assumption that the supplies of domestic and foreign assets are exogenous. However, see the summary of the results of Dornbusch and Fischer (1980) and Rodriguez (1980) that will be presented later.

with asset participation in world markets would be expected to experience the larger exchange-rate fluctuation.[5]

Given the dynamics of the model, it is evident that the asset market determines the exchange rate in the short run, whereas the current account determines the exchange rate in the long run.[6] The speed of adjustment is itself a function of the relative sizes of trade and capital flows. In a simulation, with the sum of the export and import elasticities with respect to the exchange rate equal to 2, Kouri found that if the level of investment was 50 percent of the level of trade, the weight of the long-run exchange rate in the average exchange rate was 57 percent in the first year following a disturbance and 94 percent in the second year. However, if investment were twice the level of trade, the long-run exchange rate would have a weight of only 21 percent in the first year and 52 percent in the second; it would require 4.6 years for the market to eliminate 90 percent of the initial deviation from long-run equilibrium (Kouri, 1978, p. 29).[7]

The Kouri model has been extended along several interesting lines. Dornbusch and Fischer (1980) developed the analysis in a general-equilibrium context, linking the current-account balance more explicitly with savings behavior as a function of desired wealth. In that dimension it moves significantly closer to the intertemporal maximization models of Helpman and Razin, while simultaneously demonstrating that Kouri's main results are not contingent on the partial-equilibrium aspects of the model. Unlike the overshooting models, in which results hinge critically on assumptions made about differing speeds of

---

[5] As was noted in Chapter 4, it can be argued that only PPP is consistent with rational expectations for the determination of the long-run-equilibrium exchange rate.

[6] Note, in particular, that it is the asset market that necessarily stabilizes the exchange rate in the short run. This aspect is of importance in analyzing exchange-rate regimes under inconvertible currencies. See Chapter 8 for further analysis.

[7] In response to an unanticipated permanent disturbance with rational expectations, the speed of adjustment is slower.

adjustment in goods and asset markets, the Dornbusch-Fischer results derive from the assumption that the short-run supply of foreign assets (the only form other than domestic money in which wealth may be held) is predetermined, in the context of price flexibility and full employment.[8]

Dornbusch and Fischer derived the acceleration hypothesis when the traded goods produced in the two countries differ. The exchange rate then becomes a terms-of-trade variable. Given the instantaneous adjustments of price levels in the two countries, so that real money balances always equal desired money balances, countries in current-account surplus are experiencing currency appreciation, and conversely, in response to an unanticipated disturbance. The exchange rate, in general, initially moves in a jump, with a once-and-for-all adjustment, followed by gradual convergence to the new, zero-current-account, level. If, for example, there were an increase in imports accompanied by a reduced domestic saving propensity, there would be an initial increase in the price of foreign exchange as the terms of trade depreciated; thereafter, the exchange rate would depreciate along a path (consistent with rational expectations) as assets were decumulated to the new equilibrium exchange rate.

Interestingly, the acceleration hypothesis no longer holds in cases in which there is an anticipated future disturbance. Suppose, for example, that from an initial equilibrium it was announced that the money supply would increase at some future date. An initial jump in the exchange rate would be followed by further gradual depreciation. With rational expectations, however, this expectation of depreciation would lower desired real balances, wealth, and spending and thus result in a current-account surplus. Under these circumstances, one would observe the converse combination from Kouri's acceleration hypothesis: A current-account surplus would be accompanied by currency depreciation, and conversely. When the money supply

---

[8] Dornbusch and Fischer noted that their results are sensitive to the assumptions made about the menu of assets available to domestic residents and foreigners.

in fact increased, exchange-rate depreciation would continue, but increased real balances, wealth, and spending would lead to a current-account deficit and decumulation of real assets until the initial (real) equilibrium was reattained.

That "anything can happen," depending on the assumptions made, is not surprising. What is perhaps disturbing about these results is that one can always explain whatever is happening by resort to an explanation involving "expectations." In the event that a current-account surplus and currency appreciation were observed, one could conclude that the foreign-exchange market was reacting to unanticipated news about contemporaneous events. If, instead, a current-account surplus were accompanied by currency depreciation, the appropriate conclusion would be that the foreign-exchange market was reacting to the expectation of a future shock. It is difficult to think of tests through which the empirical validity of these interpretations might be examined, unless one can forecast differences in the adjustment path to the long-run equilibrium.

Rodriguez (1980) also developed a model of the interaction between trade flows and the capital account in a general-equilibrium context. In many regards, his results are strikingly similar to those of Dornbusch and Fischer, and the acceleration hypothesis emerges from the model. In the Rodriguez model, as in that of Dornbusch and Fischer, stocks of domestic and foreign money held by domestic residents are predetermined variables, and the assumption of instantaneous portfolio equilibrium is sufficient to determine the short-term value of the exchange rate. However, Rodriguez parted from Dornbusch-Fischer in assuming that the trade balance has two components: an endogenous component depending on wealth, income, relative prices, and other variables, and an exogenous or "structural" component. To quote Rodriguez:

> For a small country . . . an exogenous deterioration of its terms of trade or an exogenous increase in the absorption function would act as a deterioration in the structural component of the trade-balance surplus.

Given enough time, it is reasonable to expect that the endogenous component of the trade balance would adjust so as to restore current payments equilibrium. To the extent, however, that the structure of the economy implies that such a shift in the structural component of the trade balance will be followed by a period of increased trade deficits, rational individuals will *anticipate* a decrease over time in the stock of foreign currency . . . and will therefore expect the price of foreign exchange to increase over time . . . This higher expected rate of depreciation of the exchange rate induces . . . an instantaneous desired shift . . . Since both money stocks are fixed at any instant, the current exchange rate must therefore jump in order to restore portfolio balance [Rodriguez, 1980, p. 1151].

Thus, the rational expectations of continued trade deficits and hence of asset decumulation are sufficient to trigger an instantaneous depreciation of the exchange rate. Conversely, given high capital mobility, a once-only disturbance in the trade balance would not be expected to affect the exchange rate unless it was expected to persist.

Rodriguez also introduced the concept of the normalized trade balance (NTB), defined as the ratio of the current-account surplus to the initial holdings of foreign currency (assets). Because the current-account surplus is the rate of increase in holdings of foreign assets, the NTB is the proportionate rate of increase in foreign-currency holdings. As in Kouri's model, an expression for the time path of the exchange rate is derived as a function of the NTB, which tends to zero as desired asset holdings approach actual asset holdings. The spot exchange rate exceeds its long-run value when there is a positive NTB and is below it with a negative NTB. Hence, the acceleration hypothesis holds once again. This result follows even if the current-account balance is not responsive to the exchange rate. Thus, the trade balance influences the exchange rate via its effects on wealth, spending, and other avenues quite apart from the influence of the exchange rate on the size of the trade balance, and it is possible to derive a model of exchange-rate determination in which the current account plays a crucial role in influencing the future path of the exchange rate even if the exchange rate does not directly influence the size of the current account.

It is apparent that many unanswered questions remain concerning current-account/capital-account exchange-rate interactions. Not only do results appear to be sensitive to the specification of asset choices and assumptions about the speed with which various markets clear, but there would also appear to be differences between models in the degree to which a current-account imbalance arises because of the exchange rate as determined in the asset market (either via its impact on wealth and hence on spending or via the responses of exports and imports to a change in the real exchange rate) or because current-account and capital-account demands for foreign exchange as a function of the real exchange rate simultaneously interact to determine an equilibrium exchange rate.

5.2 The exchange rate and the terms of trade

A model combining the older elasticities approach with rational expectations and a "transactions-constraint" demand for money has been developed by Stockman (1980). It focuses on the question of the real variables that enter into exchange-rate determination, in addition to PPP. It integrates many of the conclusions derived from overshooting asset models with some of the results of the older elasticities analysis of the role of the exchange rate.

Interestingly, Stockman's modeling of the monetary component of his model generated results in the context of a full equilibrium framework with fully flexible prices and all markets adjusting instantaneously. He obtained overshooting in some cases even though all prices and markets adjust instantaneously. His approach is sufficiently different from other asset-market models that several preliminary comments are in order.

First, Stockman assumed a two-country world, in which commodity 1 is produced only in country 1, and commodity 2 only in country 2.[9] Domestic prices are the price of the domestically produced good in each country and the imported good (whose price equals the foreign price times the price of foreign exchange). Thus, a change in the exchange rate (holding domestic price levels constant) potentially represents a change in the terms of trade. As the model actually operates, a change in the terms of trade (resulting from shifts in demand and supplies for different commodity bundles) is effected partly through changes in domestic price levels and partly through a change in the exchange rate.

Second, Stockman assumed a transactions constraint in deriving individual holdings of the two countries' monies. In many regards, his modeling of the asset component is closer to the original monetary-approach view than it is to the asset markets of recent years. The demand for foreign exchange is a derived demand (as in Kouri's model) reflecting individuals' demands to purchase foreign goods. Stockman used the "liquidity constraint" first developed by Clower (1967) to derive individuals' holdings of each currency from utility maximization:

> The transactions technology involves a "liquidity constraint" on individual behavior that attempts to reflect the facts that money is held between the transactions for which it is used and that transactions would be more costly without money. The liquidity constraint in this paper requires that goods be purchased with money and that this money be held before it is spent. Expenditures during any period must be financed out of money available at the beginning of the period [Stockman, 1980, p. 680].

[9] Stockman stated that the specialization assumption could be relaxed with no important change in the results. In some sense, however, his terms-of-trade findings emanate from the fact that the two currencies represent different bundles of goods.

Thus, the demand for money in country 1 reflects the holdings of its money by citizens of both country 1 and country 2, because the latter wish to import goods produced in country 1.

The model itself is straightforward. Individuals maximize the expected value of the sum of the (discounted) utilities of consumption of the two commodities over the present and all future time periods. Production of each good is exogenously given by a stochastic process. All international transactions are carried out in the exporter's currency. People wishing to import foreign goods hold positive balances of foreign exchange. Governments may alter the supplies of domestic money and/or intervene in the foreign-exchange market.

Given individuals' beliefs about future prices and incomes, government policies, and outputs, the prices of the two commodities in domestic currencies and the exchange rate are determined. Changes over time occur for two reasons: (1) There may be disturbances in the system (stochastic changes in outputs of goods or changes in money supplies and government intervention in the exchange market). (2) Individuals may alter the proportions in which they wish to hold the two monies in optimally adjusting to past disturbances and changes in expectations about the future.

In general, increases in either money supply or current income result in increases in demand for both goods and both monies. An increase in the price of the first good leads to a decrease in the quantity of it demanded, but an increase in the quantity demanded of the second good and both monies. Increases in the exchange rate (the price of country 2's currency in terms of country 1's currency) induce increases in demand for good 1 and money 1 and a decrease in demand for the second country's good and money.

In response to a real disturbance (an increase in the output, say, of the first commodity), both countries' domestic prices and the exchange rate adjust. The terms of trade generally turn against the first commodity, and the exchange rate depreciates.

In effect, the exchange rate serves to adjust the purchasing power of each country while domestic price levels adjust to provide the desired real balances in each currency. To state the conclusion another way, in response to a shift in excess demand that alters the equilibrium terms of trade, both the exchange rate and domestic prices adjust to bring about the new, equilibrium, terms of trade. In response to monetary shocks, however, the exchange rate carries the full adjustment, because no terms-of-trade change is called for.

Thus, terms-of-trade changes would be expected to be associated with exchange-rate changes insofar as real disturbances (not nominal disturbances) affect the exchange rate.[10] According to the Stockman model, British discoveries of North Sea oil would lead to an appreciation of the British pound relative to the PPP forecast.

It is important to note that a government cannot influence its terms of trade in the Stockman model. Even though rational individuals might perceive a relationship between exchange-rate changes and terms-of-trade changes, exchange-rate changes are simply one of the avenues by which the market adjusts to warranted terms-of-trade changes. A government attempting to exploit this relationship would find its domestic price level affected, but with the exchange rate depreciating proportionately, leaving the terms of trade unchanged.

5.3 The current-account balance as intertemporal utility maximization

The Stockman model is a "real" model in the sense that money demands are derived from the demands for goods, and the exchange rate affects the relative prices of foreign and domestic goods. Two recent papers by Razin (1980) and Helpman and Razin (1981) have also focused on "real" variables,

---

[10] Money-supply changes yield proportionate effects on the exchange rate and the ratio of the two domestic prices. The exchange rate responds also to changes in the terms of trade and therefore has greater variance than the ratio of the two nominal prices.

but of an entirely different type. Interestingly, at a time when the theory of exchange-rate determination is in some respects becoming almost a branch of monetary theory, Razin's model has focused only on determinants of the real exchange rate and its evolution over time. Helpman and Razin (1981) have worked out the interactions between the nominal and real exchange rates along the adjustment path. Using an intertemporal utility-maximization framework, they have regarded the current-account balance as the outcome of divergences in discount rates between countries; the real exchange rate (defined as the price of tradable goods relative to nontradable goods) adjusts in response to this time preference, and resources move between production of tradables and production of nontradables in response.

These models have some assumptions in common with the Stockman model. There is intertemporal utility maximization in the context of price flexibility and instantaneous adjustment in all markets. Perfect foresight, which is rational expectations under certainty, is assumed. The Helpman-Razin paper, in addition, employs the Clower transactions-constraint approach to modeling the holding of national monies.

In the Helpman-Razin approach, differences between the foreign and home rates of time preferences and between governments' spending behaviors govern the evolution of the current account. Suppose, for example, that foreigners have a lower rate of time preference than do domestic residents, while both domestic money supplies are constant. At a common rate of interest, foreign spending will increase over time while home spending declines. The foreign country is initially in current-account surplus, which declines over time. Increased spending in the foreign country implies an increasing demand for non-traded goods, which in turn implies that the relative price of nontradables must be rising (i.e., that its real exchange rate must appreciate). In turn, this implies a higher domestic-currency price for nontradables, leaving smaller currency balances for tradables and thus a drop in their absolute price (given a constant money supply) contrasted with that obtaining under a lower level of spending. As nominal prices move in the opposite direction in the home country, the exchange rate must depreciate (from the viewpoint of the foreign country) at a rate in excess of the absolute rate of change of price levels in either country. In the context of growing money supplies, these same results hold when the statements are amended to read "relative to the rate of relative domestic monetary growth."

It should be noted that the rate of change in the exchange rate is not equal to the difference in the rates of change of the two money supplies. PPP fails to hold because of the changing relative prices of tradables to nontradables and the consequent exchange-rate adjustments that occur.[11]

In the Helpman-Razin formulation, anticipated increases in the money supply do not affect the real exchange rate. An anticipated increase in the money supply increases the exchange rate in the period when it occurs, but does not affect the exchange rate in periods when there is no increase in the money supply.[12] The effects of unanticipated increases in the money supply arise only because they affect the value of real international indebtedness, which of course accompanies the evolution of current-account surpluses and deficits over time.

In the Razin model, the real exchange rate from the viewpoint of a single country is the price of tradable goods relative to nontradables. Between countries, the exchange rate equates the prices of tradables. When desired spending within a country increases, the relative price of nontradables must increase to induce a shift of production toward nontradables. Because spending on tradables must also rise (both because of the

---

[11] The rate of monetary growth equals the rate of price increase as measured by the GNP deflator; it exceeds the rate of growth of the CPI deflator when the current account is in deficit, and conversely.

[12] That this can arise and not present profit-making opportunities comes about because bonds are assumed to be short term. Adjustment in domestic nominal interest rates ensures that domestic and foreign bonds have equal yields after allowing for exchange-rate appreciation or depreciation.

increase in the level of expenditure and because the relative price of tradables falls), the current account unequivocally goes into deficit. In the context of intertemporal utility maximization, current-account imbalances are the way in which countries can trade differences in time preferences, and the real exchange rate moves to reflect these differences. As Razin pointed out, "capital movements induce fluctuations in relative prices of tradables in terms of nontradables, whereas they are likely to reduce fluctuations in world relative prices within tradable goods according to the Laursen-Metzler argument" (Razin, 1980, p. 12).

5.4 Conclusions

All three types of models surveyed in this chapter attempt to grapple with the relationship between current-account and capital-account transactions and their role in exchange-rate determination. Despite the fact that each is a full-employment, flexible-price model, their emphases are significantly different. Although none of these authors would be willing to answer the question "What does the exchange rate do?" unless permitted to specify the source of any variation in the exchange rate, they all saw the exchange rate in different roles. Kouri focused on the role of the capital account in absorbing short-term current-account imbalances and on the current-account imbalances as having effects on the exchange rate and real wealth that tend to lead the current account back into balance. Stockman's approach focused much more on the real variables that might influence the equilibrium terms of trade, and the exchange rate is one of the variables through which changes in terms of trade are transmitted. Helpman and Razin saw the exchange rate as moving in response to desired differences in spending relative to income in the context of intertemporal utility maximization, and moving resources between the traded- and nontraded-goods sectors of the economy.

It will be seen in Chapter 6 that analysis of the differences between floating- and flexible-exchange-rate regimes centers in part on one's view of the role of the exchange rate. The models presented in this chapter essentially assume full price flexibility and instantaneous adjustment. By and large, the questions raised in Chapter 6 are meaningful only in the context of one or more rigidities in the adjustment process. They thus generally assume a different underlying macroeconomic situation than the one used in this chapter.

6

Alternative exchange-rate systems

In preceding chapters, our focus was on determination of the exchange rate under a floating regime and determination of the balance of payments under a fixed-rate regime. In this chapter the situation is reversed, as we shift to analyzing what differences, if any, there are in nominal and real magnitudes depending on whether a fixed or floating regime is adopted.

Comparisons of alternative exchange-rate systems have a long history. Fundamentally, economists have approached the question by viewing the monetary arrangements underlying international transactions as a means of facilitating international flows of goods and services, which in turn have been regarded as the ultimate welfare-improving phenomena. Hence, the criterion for judging alternative exchange-rate systems rested largely on the presumed degree to which each would permit the attainment of a Pareto-optimal free-trade (and capital-flow) situation. Given that criterion, the three alternatives – fixed exchange rates, floating exchange rates, and exchange control – were quickly separated into two groups. Fixed rates and floating rates were both deemed to be preferable to exchange control, because the latter was inconsistent with achieving equality between domestic and international marginal rates of transformation and substitution among commodities, and it certainly did not permit optimal intertemporal maximization.

Thus, the literature has bifurcated, with a discussion of fixed rates versus floating rates occupying the larger part of it and analyses of exchange-control systems being undertaken relatively independently using a free-trade norm as the standard. That pattern will be followed here; the fixed- and flexible-rate alternatives will be discussed in Chapters 6 and 7, and exchange-control systems will be discussed in Chapter 8.

Until the 1970s, much of the discussion of fixed rates versus floating rates really amounted to advocacy of flexible exchange rates. Economists, impatient with the periodic discrete exchange-rate changes that were the hallmark of the Bretton Woods system, contrasted the supposed workings of a market-determined, intervention-free, floating rate system with the shortcomings of a fixed-exchange-rate system under which governments were assumed to determine their monetary and fiscal policies with little regard to their international payments positions. Friedman's analysis (1953) of flexible exchange rates was the classic.

Meanwhile, work at the IMF in the late 1950s and early 1960s focused on the impacts of monetary and fiscal policies under fixed and floating exchange rates. The seminal studies on this subject by Fleming (1962) and Mundell (1960, 1963), following Meade's earlier discussion of attainment of internal- and external-balance targets, led to a large literature contrasting the effectiveness of monetary and fiscal policies on the trade balance, on levels of real income, and on other variables under various specifications of a macroeconomic model.

That work was important in its own right, and also because it pointed the way to analysis in the 1970s of the ways in which domestic economic policies function differently in a world of floating exchange rates.[1] As can be imagined, with the unsettled

---

[1] The focus in this volume is on the theory underlying analysis of the international system. For excellent analyses of how the system has in fact functioned, the interested reader should see Corden (1977), Goldstein (1980), and McKinnon (1981).

state of macroeconomic theory in general, the variety of models of macroeconomic determination against which the workings of alternative exchange-rate systems can be analyzed is enormous. To focus on the international aspects without detouring throughout the entire bewildering variety of macroeconomic theories is exceptionally difficult. In these chapters, nonetheless, the effort is made.

This chapter is addressed to these questions: To what extent does a flexible exchange rate insulate the domestic economy from disturbances? What differences are there in the functioning of an economy depending on which exchange-rate system is adopted? As will be seen, the answers hinge crucially on the nature of the assumptions made about the degree of capital mobility.

In Chapter 7 we shall then turn to certain types of assumptions about the nature of the domestic economy that depart from the neoclassical model and examine the functioning of fixed and floating rates under those assumed market imperfections. Finally, in Chapter 8, there is a review of the functioning of exchange-control systems and of the emerging literature on the problems of "opening up" that confront economies subject to exchange control as they seek to liberalize their trade and payments regime and move to a system of either fixed or floating exchange rates.

6.1 Comparisons of fixed and flexible rate systems

Before we turn to the insulation question, one preliminary must be cleared up. It has to do with the methods of comparing fixed and flexible exchange rates. Consider two possible regimes: (1) a flexible-exchange-rate regime under which the current-account balance is zero and (2) a fixed-exchange-rate regime under which the current account may differ from zero, as private individuals' excess of spending over income can be offset by the government drawing down its foreign-exchange reserves.

It is evident that any attempt to compare these regimes must somehow take into account the country's change in indebtedness: a one-period comparison of utility realized with one-period levels of consumption will generally reveal higher welfare under the fixed-exchange-rate regime if the current account is in deficit (because total domestic consumption will be higher) and lower welfare if it is in surplus. Indeed, the more overvalued the currency and the larger the current-account deficit, the larger welfare will be deemed to be.

In comparing exchange-rate systems, the situations analyzed must be comparable. However, it cannot be that the comparison is of two situations in which the current-account deficits or surpluses are identical in size,[2] for in that circumstance, the contrast is between fixed and floating rates when the exchange rate chosen happens to be the same under both regimes. Not surprisingly, welfare comparisons of these two systems would reveal the same level of welfare.

It thus becomes necessary to attempt to specify an intertemporal model under which present values of future streams, appropriately discounted, can be evaluated. Hause (1966) was among the first to formalize the intertemporal nature of the problem. In his model he assumed that under flexible exchange rates individuals would optimize the utility of their future consumption stream assuming that current prices correctly reflect the choices available to them. He then contrasted the utility attained under two alternative situations. In the first, the exchange rate clears the market in each period of time. The second involves an initial fixed exchange rate that induces individuals to consume more than their income in early time periods and then, after a discrete and unanticipated jump in the

---

[2] Reference here is to the case with neoclassical assumptions. Once price or wage rigidities are brought into the model, the situation changes, as will be seen in Chapter 7. In general, flexible rates outperform fixed rates with price (of nontraded goods) and nominal-wage rigidity, as shown by Flanders and Helpman (1978).

exchange rate, induces individuals to consume less than their income (as the country is constrained to balancing its budget intertemporally). The welfare costs of the fixed-exchange-rate system are thus the loss associated with the nonoptimal time path of consumption.

Helpman and Razin (1979) extended the analysis to a full intertemporal optimization model in which current-account surpluses and deficits permit the community to attain preferred time paths of consumption streams relative to the optimum attainable under autarky. They pointed out that welfare under fixed exchange rates may be found to be higher than under flexible rates, if the comparison is between a floating-exchange-rate regime in which the current account always balances and a fixed-exchange-rate regime under which current-account deficits and surpluses may occur.

The reason for this is straightforward: The assumptions about the possibilities of intertemporal borrowing are not symmetric. By assumption of current-account clearing at each instant under flexible rates, the set of attainable time paths of consumption is smaller than that under fixed rates, with the implicit assumption that current-account deficits and surpluses may be incurred. This is essentially the same result as that found by Kareken and Wallace (1977) when they investigated what they termed "portfolio autarky."

Thus, Helpman and Razin (1979) concluded that "consistent" comparison requires an evaluation when the same borrowing–lending possibilities exist under both regimes. On the basis of those assumptions, and specifying money as an argument of the utility function, they found that

> there is a floating exchange rate equilibrium allocation which is preferred to every fixed exchange rate equilibrium allocation. The equilibrium is attained when a country pursues an optimal interest rate policy. In a fixed exchange rate regime countries cannot pursue independent interest rate policies, and a country which

pegs its exchange rate ends up importing the monetary inefficiency that exists abroad [Helpman and Razin, 1979, p. 405].

Seen in this light, consistent comparison of fixed versus flexible exchange rates entails examining the time path of the current-account surplus over time, which can be done only when there is a possibility of borrowing.[3] This involves the use of an explicit intertemporal utility-maximization model and examination of the behavior of maximizing individuals over time (and the consequent time path of the current-account balance). The feasible pattern of current-account balances across different states of nature becomes the criterion for evaluation. The exchange-rate regime yielding the wider choice, subject to an overall intertemporal budget constraint, is deemed to permit higher attainable welfare, as shown clearly by Helpman and Razin (1980).

To be sure, there are complications in the real world with which consistent comparisons may fail to deal adequately. In contemporary discussions of worldwide inflation, for example, the abandonment of fixed exchange rates is often bemoaned. It is assumed, either explicitly or implicitly, that under fixed exchange rates countries would have applied more restrictive monetary and fiscal policies, with a lower rate of worldwide inflation and less variation in inflation rates among countries than has occurred under floating rates. Such a comparison posits two differences: a different exchange-rate regime and a different money-supply process emanating from it. If, instead, fixed exchange rates implied exchange controls, with the same divergence in inflation rates as has in fact been realized, analysts would agree that flexible rates were the preferred alternative. One can interpret much of the current policy debate between advocates and opponents of floating rates as originat-

---

[3] Fischer (1977) had earlier contrasted the functioning of alternative regimes when subject to various shocks, recognizing that the role of capital mobility that he assumed away under flexible exchange rates might be of importance (see Section 6.2).

ing in different assumptions about the relationship of the
exchange-rate regime to the money-supply process.

As it stands, the literature on comparison of fixed and flexible
rates does not really address the issue of the degree of discipline
enforced on government under alternative regimes, except in
the sense that assuming that there is an intertemporal budget
constraint to which the government is subject may already be
assuming greater awareness of the intertemporal budget constraint than governments demonstrate. Thus, the irrationalities
associated with maintenance of a fixed exchange rate between
the deutschemark and the lira, over a period in which the rates
of price increases in the two countries diverged by about 8 percent per year, have not been addressed in the comparison question.[4] To be sure, this raises many of the questions dealt with in
the following chapters: How can there be fixed exchange rates
with divergent rates of inflation?

6.2 Insulation properties of alternative systems

The early argument for flexible exchange rates had as
one of its key points the proposition that economies would be
more fully insulated from foreign disturbances under flexible
rates than under fixed rates. This proposition generally rested
on a relatively simple Keynesian model of the determination of
the levels of output and employment by aggregate demand and
the assumption that the exchange rate would move to equate
current-account expenditures and receipts. This latter ignored
the possibility of current-account imbalance. Thereby, foreign
disturbances in the form of changes in the demand for home-
country exports could not, it was reasoned, be fed through (with
a multiplier) to the level of domestic economic activity.

As late as 1969, Harry Johnson could argue that "the fundamental argument for flexible exchange rates is that they
allow countries autonomy with respect to their use of monetary,

---

[4] Nor does the literature deal with the problems that arise from the
existence of negative real rates of interest that sometimes accompany inflation.

fiscal, and other policy instruments, consistent with the maintenance of whatever degree of freedom in international transactions they choose to allow their citizens" (Johnson, 1970, p. 12). Whereas some, including most notably Robert Mundell, have used the insulation property to argue that flexible exchange rates have permitted worldwide inflation and that fixed rates are preferable because they prevent it, a large literature has emerged examining the circumstances under which, and the extent to which, the insulation properties of flexible- and fixed-exchange-rate systems differ. Clearly, insulation can occur only when it is assumed that flexible rates maintain constancy of the current-account balance.

Even in older, current-account models there was one exception noted with respect to the insulation properties of flexible exchange rates: that is, a shift in world terms of trade. An adverse shift in the terms of trade would, according to Harberger (1950) and Laursen and Metzler (1950), reduce real income and hence real savings. Consequently, the ex-ante current-account balance would deteriorate for a given level of investment, and the exchange rate would depreciate to restore equilibrium. Recently, again in the framework of an intertemporal utility-maximizing model, Svensson and Razin (1981) have challenged this result, noting that a permanent deterioration in the terms of trade is a reduction in expected present and future real income: The response of savings in the current period to this reduction is indeterminate.

The Harberger-Laursen-Metzler effect arose even under the assumption that only current-account transactions were at issue, which was the context of the discussion of fixed and flexible exchange rates in the 1950s and early 1960s. As was seen in Chapter 3, Mundell, Fleming, and others challenged the insulation property of flexible exchange rates simply by introducing a capital-flows response to changes in interest differentials. Thus, in the Mundell-Fleming assignment models, a foreign monetary disturbance could be fed directly into the domestic level of economic activity under flexible exchange rates, because a change in the foreign interest rate would induce capital flows, which in turn would induce a change in the exchange rate in order to induce the current account to move in the direction opposite to the capital-account movement.

The insulation issue is addressed solely to the question whether or not external disturbances will be transmitted to the internal market, and to what degree. It is perfectly possible for insulation to be highly imperfect and simultaneously for internal disturbances to cause far larger variance in the relevant variables than external disturbances. Thus, the insulation question is not the same as this question: Under what circumstances will the variance in domestic variable x be smaller: fixed or flexible exchange rates? Indeed, it is likely that with a high degree of insulation under flexible rates, internal disturbances will be transmitted abroad more readily under fixed rates. Therefore, it is possible that a fixed-exchange-rate regime would provide a lower level of total variance for the domestic economy if internal disturbances had a significantly higher coefficient of variation than external disturbances.[5]

This sort of mechanism was modeled by Fischer (1977), who, in a monetarist model of the balance of payments, with real output a random variable, examined the variance in monetary and real variables in response to domestic and foreign disturbances under fixed and flexible rates. As mentioned in Section 6.1, he assumed an absence of capital flows, which is an important qualification to the results. For internal disturbances, he found that under floating rates all adjustments were in prices, with none in quantities, whereas under fixed rates the opposite pairing held. For external disturbances, the results were similar: Foreign-price-level disturbances affected only the exchange rate under floating rates; under fixed rates, both the domestic price

---

[5] In fact, the Mundell argument for a return to fixed exchange rates is tantamount to asserting that domestic disturbances are the primary source of inflation in most countries, although the exchange-rate system is also assumed to influence the money supply in the degree of discipline imposed. For a balanced discussion of this issue, see Corden (1977, Chapters 4 and 5).

level and the level of real consumption were affected by foreign disturbances.[6]

Formally, the insulation problem is the question of the circumstances under which disturbances in the foreign economy are transmitted to the domestic economy. The degree of insulation, I, is generally defined as

$$I = 1 - dV/d\overline{V} \qquad (6.1)$$

where dV is the change in the magnitude of the domestic variable V and $\overline{V}$ is the corresponding foreign variable that was altered. When the variable of interest is the domestic price level, P,

$$I = 1 - dP/d\overline{P} \qquad (6.1')$$

and insulation is said to be complete ($I = 1$) when the exchange rate moves so as to offset movements in the foreign price level.[7]

When interest focuses on real magnitudes, the relation is more complex, and V and $\overline{V}$ may be expressed in proportionate terms or as weighted averages of the variables of interest. Often, there is no single, well-defined degree of insulation for all variables and disturbances.

Usually, one can distinguish nominal and real disturbances, and the degrees of insulation may well differ systematically between the two types but be alike within types. Under fixed exchange rates, monetary disturbances abroad that affect capital-account transactions are unlikely to filter through to the domestic real variables, whereas under flexible exchange rates changes in the capital account that generate changes in the real exchange rate obviously preclude full insulation. Under the monetary approach to the balance of payments, for example,

---

[6] Lapan and Enders (1980) extended the Fischer results in an overlapping-generations framework, still under the asymmetric assumption that flexible exchange rates imply a zero current-account deficit, whereas fixed rates permit nonzero current-account deficits. They found it necessary to distinguish individual utility levels from the variability of aggregate consumption.

[7] Van Duyne (1980) provided a straightforward analysis of this case.

with its law-of-one-price equation, equation (4.2), fixed exchange rates provide full insulation from domestic monetary disturbances, but foreign-price-level disturbances are fully transmitted.

For modern asset-market approaches to exchange-rate determination, as well as models of capital-account and current-account interaction, the issue becomes one of when instantaneous adjustment of the exchange rate permits domestic nominal and real variables to remain unaltered. Obviously, in any of the overshooting models, whether because of rigidities in adjustments in goods markets (Dornbusch, 1976) or because of expectations, changes in the real exchange rate in response to an external disturbance affect both nominal and real variables, and insulation is incomplete. Recently, Van Duyne (1980) has argued that even in the case of foreign price disturbances, insulation is incomplete under flexible exchange rates whenever a wealth effect or less-than-perfect foresight is present.

In current-account/capital-account models of the Kouri or Allen-Kenen type, the short-run exchange rate is determined in the asset market only. Anything that impinges on the net excess supply and demand for assets will prevent complete insulation of the domestic economy, whereas goods-market disturbances will leave the domestic economy unaffected in the short run. In the long run, the opposite result may hold, because real variables will adjust to the altered exchange rate, and other variables may, depending on the model, return to their initial values (see Section 6.3).

Turnovsky considered additional aspects of the insulation question. In a dynamic model with accumulation of real wealth, changing money stock, changing terms of trade, and perfect myopic foresight (under which the expected rates of inflation and exchange-rate changes are realized in the evolution of the system, but may themselves change over time), Turnovsky (1979*a*) addressed the insulation question for two fully anticipated situations: a permanent increase in the foreign steady-state rate of inflation and a once-and-for-all increase in the foreign price level. Essentially, the results are similar to those reported earlier: For an increase in the foreign steady-state rate of inflation, flexible exchange rates can provide full insulation whenever the changed foreign rate of inflation leaves all real foreign variables (including the real rate of interest) unaffected.

For a once-and-for-all increase in the foreign price level, however, the degree of insulation is generally less than complete, with relatively stringent conditions for short-run full insulation (domestic residents do not hold foreign assets, or else the domestic demand for money is independent of the domestic interest rate and has a unit wealth elasticity) and a possibility of zero insulation (which becomes even more likely if exchange-rate expectations are static).

To investigate unanticipated disturbances, Turnovsky (1979b) used a stochastic model of a small open economy and analyzed its response to a domestic monetary expansion and a foreign price disturbance. His conclusion, indicating the sensitivity of the insulation problem to model specification, is worth quoting:

> When these factors are all taken into account, any given monetary disturbance can generate a variety of short-run effects, depending upon the accuracy with which it is predicted and how it causes expectations to be revised. It may be associated with overshooting or undershooting of the exchange rate . . . and may even have perverse short-run effects on output [Turnovsky, 1979b, p. 33].

With respect to foreign price changes, Turnovsky found that insulation was only partial as long as foreign securities were held in domestic residents' portfolios, even when the price change was expected to be permanent. In the event of transitory price increases, insulation was generally incomplete.

In a sense, all the questions to be addressed later with respect to the impact of alternative government policies under fixed and flexible exchange rates can be interpreted as variants on the insulation question. Whenever a domestic policy is found to be totally ineffective (as, for example, under fixed exchange rates and Mundell-type capital flows, when the money supply is increased), the rest of the world is not insulated with respect to a domestic disturbance.

6.3 The managed float

Early discussions of fixed versus floating rates implicitly assumed that the policy choice would be either pure fixity or pure flexibility. In this context, analyses such as that of Fischer tended to investigate the type of regime – fixed or flexible – that would minimize disturbances for various kinds of shocks.[8]

Recently, analysis has shifted to investigating the optimal degree of intervention in the foreign-exchange market, where zero intervention is synonymous with flexible exchange rates and full intervention is a regime of fixed exchange rates.

In a large simulation exercise, Kenen (1975) examined alternative indicator rules, including fixed and flexible rates, temporary floats, and monthly setting of the exchange rate at a moving average of the equilibrium rate. He found that rules based on averages of past market rates and on changes in reserves tended to be more efficient in minimizing exchange-rate fluctuations and trade-volume variability.

Frenkel (1980*b*) developed a simple model of a small economy subject to two types of shocks, one to the supply of domestic output (the real shock) and one to the monetary sector. It is assumed that PPP and the law of one price continuously hold, so that relative prices are not affected by exchange-rate changes. Solving for the exchange-rate changes that would prevail under fixed rates and under flexible rates in response to these shocks, he derived an "intervention coefficient," γ, the coefficient of managing a float. When $\gamma = 0$, exchange rates are fixed, and when $\gamma = 1$ it is a fully floating system. In the

---

[8] For a survey of the literature, see Tower and Willett (1976).

Frenkel model, one would let the exchange rate correct monetary shocks but hold the exchange rate fixed against real shocks if the source of the disturbance were known. However, if it is only the joint outcome of the two disturbances that is known, rather than the sources of disturbances individually, a managed float becomes a second-best optimal policy.

Frenkel found that optimal policy would generally lie in partial intervention, with fixed rates being optimal only when the only shocks are real, and flexible rates being optimal only when the shocks are all monetary. The degree of intervention should be greater, the higher the variance of the real shock and the lower the variance of the monetary shock. To be sure, the rationale for government intervention must still rest on the presumption that government policymakers have information superior to that available from the private sector, as Frenkel noted. Nor does the proposition that some intervention might be optimal prove that the managed floating actually practiced since 1973 has been optimal. Exchange market intervention that fully offsets shifts in supply and demand for foreign exchange can never be optimal, and, in the Frenkel model, perverse intervention, in which the authorities buy or sell enough foreign exchange to move the exchange rate in the direction opposite to that in which it would otherwise go, can never be optimal.

A "targets, instruments, and indicators" approach to optimal exchange-rate intervention was modeled by Boyer (1978). Following recent developments in monetary theory, wherein the target variable is contemporaneously unobservable, and wherein instrument variables must be employed in response to indicators that are correlated with the target variable, Boyer modeled optimal foreign-exchange intervention. In his model there are two markets: domestic money and domestic goods. Shocks may arise in both markets and may be positively or negatively correlated. The authorities have only one target variable, namely, the level of output, which is assumed to be contemporaneously unobservable. Intervention can take place in the foreign-exchange market either through buying or selling goods or through buying or selling assets.[9] Intervention in the money market takes place through open-market operations that trade traded bonds for domestic money.

In the case in which shocks arise only in one market, Boyer concluded that

> the optimal policy is to peg the exchange rate if shocks arise in the market of intervention. If shocks arise in the intervention-free market instead, it is optimal to design intervention so as to offset the effects the exchange rate has upon private sector excess demand, so that the combined demand in the market of intervention is independent of the indicator variable [Boyer, 1978, p. 1051].

When shocks occur in both markets, the result depends on the sign of the correlation between them. When the correlation is negative, optimal policy calls for less than complete pegging of the exchange rate and operating the intervention market to keep excess demand independent of the indicator variable. When the correlation is positive, managed floating is optimal. However, if the correlation between shocks is sufficiently large, it is even possible that managed intervention could be perverse and could move the exchange rate in the direction opposite to the direction it would take in the absence of intervention.

It is of interest to note that Boyer's results are very similar to the Mundell-Fleming conclusions on the efficacy of fiscal and monetary policies under alternative exchange-rate systems, when intervention takes place in the money market, the usual "asset" assumption. However, if intervention in determining the exchange rate takes place through the goods market (opposite to the usual assumptions), the results are reversed.

As these considerations show, Boyer's analysis alters some of

---

[9] The goods-market assumptions are virtually equivalent to assuming that intervention takes place through the imposition or removal of tariffs, export subsidies, and other commercial policy instruments, which Boyer saw as constituting a "close substitute" for changes in the exchange rate (Boyer, 1978, p. 1049).

the previously held views. Earlier discussions of insulation and related issues tended to identify optimal intervention strategies with the geographic source of the disturbance (domestic or foreign). Boyer's conclusions, instead, focus on the relative importance of shocks in the market of intervention relative to other markets, with the degree of correlation between disturbances also influencing optimal intervention; in general, some degree of foreign-exchange market intervention will prove to be optimal and will require intervention in only one market if there is only one target.[10]

6.4 Impact of fiscal and monetary policies

In this section, the impact of monetary and fiscal policies is examined under the assumption that real output increases in response to increases in aggregate demand, either directly or because increased demand leads to higher prices that induce output increases. This assumption is consistent with Lucas-type supply functions, under which individuals are misled into believing that price increases for their product reflect relative price changes, whereas they are in fact part of the inflationary process. Alternatively, it is consistent with the assumption that the nominal wage adjusts sluggishly or is fixed in the short run for institutional reasons, or that aggregate demand determines output as in the older Keynesian models.

Obviously, the ways in which monetary and fiscal policies impinge on an economy depend in large part on the underlying assumptions with regard to that economy. If real output fluctuates with aggregate demand, macroeconomic disturbances affect the overall level of output. If a class of nontraded goods exists, any movement in the real exchange rate (the price of traded goods in terms of home goods) can be presumed to have some effect on resource allocation and consumption decisions within the domestic economy.

---

[10] Kenen (1975) pointed out that there is an analogy between Boyer's conclusions and the welfare results of trade theory in the case of a distortion: First-best policy will be an intervention in the market closest to the distortion.

Results also hinge crucially on the underlying model of exchange-rate determination. When the asset market determines the instantaneous exchange rate, disturbances (or policies) must impinge on that market for their impact effect, and changes in the real exchange rate then result from those asset-market changes.

In the following sections the short-run impacts of monetary and fiscal policies at home and abroad will be examined under fixed and flexible exchange rates. The simplest case is zero capital mobility. Next, the differences under perfect capital mobility will be examined. These analyses are undertaken within the conventional context of single-period analysis. Finally, the extent to which results are altered in the long run under various models of macroeconomic activity and exchange-rate determination will be considered. Mussa has provided a nice synthesis of various models, and his exposition is essentially followed in Sections 6.4.1 and 6.4.2. Throughout, the following model of a domestic economy is assumed:

$$Q = Q(P/W) \quad \left(\frac{\partial Q}{\partial (P/W)} > 0 \right) \tag{6.2}$$

$$M^d = M^s \tag{6.3}$$

$$\frac{M^d}{P} = M^d(i, Q, A) \tag{6.4}$$

where A is real domestic wealth held by residents, M is money, with d and s denoting demand and supply, Q is real home output, i is nominal interest rate, P is the price of domestic output,[11] and W is the domestic nominal wage rate. When needed, the same structure will be assumed for the foreign country, or rest of the world, and asterisks are used to denote foreign variables. Equation (6.2) is the aggregate (domestic) supply function. Equation (6.3) asserts that the money market clears (there is implicitly a bond market in the system, but it is not necessary at this juncture), and (6.4) is the traditional demand-for-money

---

[11] PPP does not necessarily hold in this model.

equation, as a function of prices, the interest rate, and the level of real domestic output.

Desired domestic expenditures, E, measured in units of national output, are a function of real national income, Y, the real rate of interest, r, real domestic wealth, and a shift parameter, g, which can be used to represent the impact of fiscal policy or an exogenous change in desired domestic expenditure:

$$E = E(Y, r, A; g) \quad \left(0 < \frac{\partial E}{\partial Y} < 1; \frac{\partial E}{\partial g} = 1 \right) \quad (6.5)$$

It is assumed that nationals of each country have a marginal preference for their own goods, an assumption compatible with the presence of a home good or with the notion of different output bundles. The real rate of interest equals the nominal rate less the expected rate of inflation, π, and real national income equals real national output plus the real rate of interest on the net domestic holding of foreign bonds:

$$r = i - \pi \tag{6.6}$$
$$Y = A + r(b - \bar{b}) \tag{6.7}$$

where b is domestically held bonds and $\bar{b}$ is domestically issued bonds.

Thus, domestic desired expenditures increase with domestic real output, the domestic supply of money, domestic holdings of bonds, domestic wealth, and the expected rate of inflation (because the real rate of interest declines).

Imports, I, are an increasing function of the desired level of expenditures and a decreasing function of the relative price of foreign output in terms of domestic output, T:

$$I = I(E, T) \quad \left(\frac{\partial I}{\partial E} > 0, \frac{\partial I}{\partial T} < 0 \right) \tag{6.8}$$

The trade balance, B, is simply

$$B = TI^* - I \tag{6.9}$$

For domestic macroeconomic equilibrium, demand for national output must equal supply. The demand for the home country's output, D, equals domestic expenditures.

$$D = E + B \tag{6.10}$$

6.4.1 *Short-run effects under capital immobility*

Consider first flexible exchange rates. Because the trade balance must always be zero in the absence of capital flows, each country's production of output must equal the demand for its output. Because that demand, in turn, is a function only of domestic variables, insulation is complete.[12] Stated another way, a change in the shift parameter, g, affects E, and therefore Q, but it does not spill over into the other country's market. If, for example, there is expansionary monetary policy in the foreign country, its output and desired expenditure level will increase, as will its demand for imports. But the increased demand for imports will result in a depreciating exchange rate (from the viewpoint of the foreign country). By assumption of a single domestic output, the insulation from foreign disturbances on the overall level of economic activity is complete.[13]

Under fixed exchange rates, however, changes in official reserves can offset trade-account imbalances. The expenditure function of each country hinges on output levels in both countries, and the (fixed) exchange rate is a parameter of the expenditure function. Thus, if there is increased desired expenditure in the foreign country (an upward shift in g^*, due, say, to fiscal policy), the demand for home output increases, and the equilibrium level of home output rises, as part of the upward shift in desired expenditure abroad spills over into the domestic market.

---

[12] That is, g^* is not an argument of the reduced form of E under flexible rates.

[13] If there were assumed to be a nontraded good in each country, an appreciation of the real exchange-rate change would induce a changed composition of output and consumption, with more traded goods and fewer home goods being produced and consumed in the new equilibrium.

When the level of output is fixed (under strictly neoclassical conditions, for example), the analysis can be carried through unaltered, except that insulation-property questions pertain to the price level rather than to levels of real output. Thus, if there is an upward shift in desired expenditure abroad under flexible rates, the consequent increase in price level is entirely borne by the foreign country. From the home country's viewpoint, the exchange rate appreciates enough to insulate the domestic economy. Under fixed exchange rates, of course, foreign prices and domestic prices must both increase in response to an upward shift in desired expenditures in either country.

The only difference between output increases engendered by monetary policy and those engendered by fiscal policy in the capital-immobility case originates in the mechanism by which they are transmitted to desired expenditures. With expansionary monetary policy in the home country, that country's interest rate declines, which induces the expenditure increase. With fiscal policy, expenditures increase automatically, and the interest rate must rise if the money supply remains constant. It is this difference that is the basis of the analysis of the effects of monetary and fiscal policies under capital mobility.

6.4.2 *Short-run effects under perfect capital mobility*

Under perfect capital mobility, the interest rate must be the same in the home country as in the rest of the world.[14] Demand for each country's output is a function of home output, foreign output, and the exchange rate.

Determination of equilibrium, and the impact of policies, can be understood with the aid of Figure 6.1, taken from the work of Mussa. Starting with the flexible-exchange-rate case, the *ee* line, found by varying the exchange rate, represents the combinations of outputs of the two countries that are consistent with demand equaling supply for each output. At a lower price of

---

[14] Strictly speaking, there could also be a constant differential in interest rates, and capital could still be mobile.

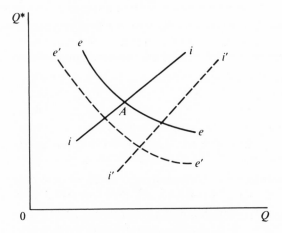

Figure 6.1. The capital-mobility case.

foreign exchange, the demand for home-country output (Q) will be lower, and therefore the level of real output lower, than with a higher price of foreign exchange. Thus, as home output increases, the exchange rate depreciates from the viewpoint of the home country, and foreign output falls, yielding the downward-sloping line *ee* in Figure 6.1.

To determine world equilibrium along the *ee* line, the additional condition is that the domestic interest rate must equal that abroad. The equilibrium output combinations consistent with this requirement are given by the *ii* line in Figure 6.1. An increase in home output increases the home demand for money and thus is consistent with an increase in the home interest rate. Because interest rates must be equalized, this is possible only when foreign output also rises. The conditions of equilibrium (demand for each country's output equaling the level of output, and equality of the interest rates) are satisfied at point A in Figure 6.1.[15]

---

[15] To simplify analysis, it is assumed that the trade balance is zero at this point and net holdings of foreign bonds are zero, so that output equals income in each country.

It is apparent that a change in expenditure in either country does not directly affect the *ii* line in Figure 6.1. It does, however, affect the *ee* curve. In particular, a reduction in foreign expenditures, g^*, shifts the *ee* curve to the new *e'e'* line in Figure 6.1: The same level of foreign output can be achieved only with a higher relative price of goods from the home country (and thus with lower home-country output), and a given level of home output is consistent with lower output in the rest of the world than before the shift. The reason for this is that reduced foreign output lowers foreign demand for home goods and foreign demand for money. The resulting current-account surplus (from the viewpoint of the foreign country), which was offset by exchange-rate depreciation under capital immobility, is largely accommodated by a capital movement, so that the new equilibrium is consistent with a current-account imbalance. Thus, the effect of a foreign macroeconomic disturbance is, under flexible exchange rates, transmitted to the home country via the possibility of trade imbalances financed by capital flows.

By contrast, a change in either money supply (monetary policy) directly affects the *ii* line, as well as the *ee* line. Because a decrease in the foreign money supply directly decreases the desired level of expenditures on both home and foreign goods, the shift in *ee* is downward as before. In addition, however, the reduction in the foreign money supply tends to raise the interest rate in the foreign country, further depressing foreign expenditures while inducing a capital flow from the home country to the foreign country. This leads to an appreciation of the foreign currency (depreciation of the home currency), which further depresses the level of output abroad, but tends to raise it at home. The new equilibrium, as shown in Figure 6.1, is a much-reduced level of output in the foreign country and increased levels of output and income in the home country.

The difference between the impacts of monetary policies and fiscal policies under flexible rates and capital mobility comes about because of the induced capital flow. Indeed, if one attempted to explain the source of the reduction in the foreign money supply by an action such as an open-market purchase of bonds, the assumption of perfect capital mobility would imply that home-country residents would be selling bonds to foreigners as fast as the foreign Central Bank tried to absorb them. The effect on the exchange rate of the resulting capital flow would imply that the current account must shift in the opposite direction to restore equilibrium. Hence the famous Mundell conclusion that under flexible exchange rates, monetary policy will be considerably more potent to affect the level of economic activity than under fixed exchange rates, whereas fiscal policy will be somewhat less potent.

In the case of fixed exchange rates with capital mobility, the only difference from the analysis with immobility is that any incipient change in interest rates that would occur under capital immobility is reflected in a redistribution of the world's money stock and assets. If, for example, fiscal policy under fixed rates would tend to raise the interest rate (because the demand for money would increase with a higher level of domestic income and output), then under capital mobility the same disturbance would lead to less of an increase in the interest rate at home (because of capital outflows) and an increase in the interest rate abroad. The latter would tend to reduce somewhat the foreign level of output, thereby offsetting part of the increase that would otherwise occur because of increased demand for the foreigners' goods by domestic residents. Thus, with fixed exchange rates, less of the increase in expenditure emanating from domestic fiscal policy is likely to spill over into foreigners' goods markets under capital mobility than under capital immobility. Hence, capital mobility increases the degree of insulation of the rest of the world to domestic-goods market disturbances under fixed exchange rates and reduces it under flexible exchange rates.

By contrast, capital mobility increases the extent to which monetary disturbances spill over from one country to another under fixed exchange rates. This follows straightforwardly from the proposition that under capital mobility an increase in the domestic money supply must be reflected in an immediate capital outflow, which in turn is likely to reduce interest rates in the rest of the world. Under capital mobility and flexible exchange rates, a monetary disturbance in a given country results in a trade imbalance for that country, so that there is, in fact, negative transmission of the original disturbance. If, for example, the home country attempts to increase its money supply, the consequent capital outflow and current-account deficit increase home output and income by more than would occur in a closed economy, whereas output and income in the rest of the world will decline.

The proposition that the potency and relative effectiveness of monetary and fiscal policies are altered under flexible exchange rates is important for interpreting the events of the 1970s. The fact that the degree of capital mobility also significantly affects their functioning further suggests that care must be taken in predicting the impacts of monetary and fiscal policies in the post–Bretton Woods world of flexible exchange rates and a fairly high degree of capital mobility.

6.4.3 *Long-run effects*

The analysis of the preceding two subsections was carried out in the conventional "flow" context of the 1960s. Once it is recognized that capital flows or official reserve movements affect the sizes of stocks, that analysis must be regarded as short-run in nature, and long-term modifications resulting from asset changes must be considered. Here, attention turns to the long-run implications of shocks under alternative exchange-rate systems for some of the approaches surveyed in Chapters 4 and 5.

Take the case of capital immobility first. There, the impact and steady-state effects of shocks under flexible exchange may be considered the same: No stocks are affected because the current-account balance is always zero, and there are no holdings of foreign-currency assets. In the fixed-exchange-rate case, however, there are implicitly flows of reserve assets between governments that affect the sizes of stocks. Moreover, under the monetary approach to the balance of payments, those changes in reserve assets result in changes in the domestic money supply. Even if sterilization is possible, maintenance of a fixed exchange rate in the longer run must imply some adjustment within at least the domestic economy incurring the decrease in reserve-asset holdings, for otherwise those assets would eventually reach zero, and the system would have to change.

When money stocks adjust in response to current-account imbalances financed by flows of reserve assets, the interest rate rises in the country decumulating reserve assets (because the money supply decreases), thereby reducing desired expenditures, whereas the opposite happens in the current-account-surplus, reserve-asset-receiving country. This, of course, increases the extent to which an initial shock under fixed exchange rates is transmitted to the rest of the world, so that long-run insulation is less than short-run insulation.

It should be noted in passing that, given these flows, some of the Mundell-Fleming results may be reversed in the long run. Rodriguez (1979) has shown that, taking into account portfolio considerations, the increased holdings of foreign assets accompanying a monetary expansion will, once portfolio balance is achieved, imply a deterioration in the trade balance. If that is the case,

> the question arises as to whether in the long run a monetary expansion, which deteriorates the trade balance, may not actually induce a *fall* in income and employment; similarly, to the extent that expansionary fiscal policy works towards an improved long-run trade balance, it may be able to increase income in the long run despite its short-run ineffectiveness [Rodriguez, 1979, p. 177].

Obstfeld (1980a), in a similar model, assumed imperfect asset substitutability. He showed that monetary policy might exert an independent influence under fixed exchange rates (due to wealth effects) and that government debt can make monetary effects nonneutral, even in the long run.

Thus, if one considers a permanent adoption of monetary or fiscal policy (as contrasted with a temporary one expected to be reversed with the next shock in economic activity), the Mundell-Fleming conclusions may be reversed once portfolio balance is reached in the long run. It could thus be that expansionary monetary policy leads to increased output in the short run and reduced output in the long run.

6.4.4 *Impact and steady-state effects*

Allen and Kenen (1980) have provided an exhaustive and systematic analysis of the response of the economy, under alternative exchange-rate systems, to various shocks in an asset model of exchange-rate determination and balance-of-payments adjustment. Using a portfolio approach similar to that of Branson for the demand for money, domestic bonds, and foreign bonds, they developed an analysis of the economy's responses to real and monetary disturbances.[16]

Their model represents a hybrid between the zero-capital-mobility and perfect-capital-mobility cases discussed earlier. Under their specification, however, the short-run adjustment of the exchange rate is entirely in response to asset-market disturbances (as in the Kouri model presented in Chapter 5). Thus, they found that

> to afford instantaneous insulation, the exchange rate must be free to adjust immediately and sufficiently to forestall any change in the current-account balance ... Two conditions must therefore be satisfied. First, disturbances affecting goods markets must have an immediate influence on asset markets. Second, a

[16] The reader interested in a systematic exposition of the asset-market approach more complete than can be given here is referred to the Allen-Kenen volume (1980), especially Chapters 1 through 6.

change in the exchange rate must not affect the capital-account balance directly.

The first condition does not hold in our model. The demands for money and bonds do not depend on income, and asset markets are cleared by the interest rate and the exchange rate. Therefore, a goods-market disturbance cannot produce immediate exchange-rate changes. With the passage of time, of course, the demand for money *is* affected, because changes in income cause saving or dissaving, altering demands for assets. But the corresponding change in the exchange rate cannot confer insulation until the steady state is reached, because the second condition is not satisfied. Any change in the exchange rate affects the home-currency value of the foreign bond and must therefore generate capital flows [Allen and Kenen, 1980, p. 95].

In general, their findings are consistent with the foregoing presentation, although the time paths to steady-state values are emphasized, and the fact that savings or dissavings (which must be reflected in wealth accumulation and therefore also foreign-asset accumulation) occur over time focuses on the time paths of adjustment to alternative disturbances. In response to a temporary tax reduction and a resulting budget deficit, for example, they found that both fixed and flexible exchange rates will raise the price of nontraded goods in the home country initially. In the steady state the price of nontradables will be unaffected under fixed exchange rates and lower under flexible rates (under the assumption that saving is relatively more sensitive to changes in wealth and that the demand for money is relatively more sensitive to changes in the interest rate). Likewise, disposable income will increase in the short run under both exchange-rate regimes, whereas it will return to its original level under fixed exchange rates and will decrease in the long run under flexible rates. Thus, in the Allen-Kenen model, most of the results of Sections 6.4.1 and 6.4.2 are found to hold, but the time frame varies depending on whether or not the disturbance impacts directly on asset markets.

6.4.5 *Expectations*

It was seen in Chapters 4 and 5 that expectations play a crucial role in affecting the response of the exchange rate or the balance of payments to various shocks. The results in the earlier parts of this section must now be modified to take those effects into account. Fortunately, however, the modifications hinge crucially only on the degree to which expectations affect the time path of the real exchange rate or the current-account path.

It should be noted first that not all assumptions are consistent with rational expectations. For example, the assumptions that a fixed exchange rate is expected to endure forever, that it is initially at an equilibrium value, and that the monetary authority alters the money supply once and for all are not mutually consistent: If the prevailing rate prior to the alteration is an equilibrium rate, and if the monetary authority's action, although unexpected, is the only shock to the system, then either there must be future changes in the reserve holdings of the Central Bank (as people adjust to their altered private asset holdings) or the exchange rate cannot persist indefinitely.

The formal role for expectations enters through modification of the interest-rate-parity condition to allow for expected changes in the exchange rate, under flexible rates, or for expected changes in asset holdings, including money, under fixed exchange rates. If a monetary or fiscal policy shift is fully anticipated, then one should expect no effect of a monetary or fiscal policy shift at the time it occurs: Any effect will have taken place at the time the policy change was announced or anticipated. If, on the other hand, there is overshooting accompanying a surprise change, the long-run effects go in the opposite direction to the initial ones spelled out earlier. The initial response is a once-and-for-all jump in the direction indicated. Thereafter, the real exchange rate and other variables move toward their new expected long-run path in the opposite direction. Long-run steady state, of course, lies in the same direction as the impact effect, but is smaller in absolute magnitude.

Turnovsky (1981) recently discussed many of these results, developing a stochastic model in which domestic agents form expectations about possible changes in variables. He then analyzed the effects of devaluation and foreign-price-level disturbances within this framework. In general, the degree to which changes impact on the domestic economy depends crucially on the degree to which they are anticipated (in which case there is no contemporaneous effect apart from whatever time path the variables are following on their way to long-run equilibrium) and the degree to which they are expected to be permanent. Thus, it is only the unanticipated component of a devaluation or foreign-price-level disturbance that has effects on real variables at the time at which the event occurs.

7

Policy effects under differing macroeconomic specifications

It has already been seen in preceding chapters that analysis of alternative exchange-rate regimes depends critically on the underlying macroeconomic structure of the economy, the assumed links between asset and goods markets, and the formation of expectations. In the last chapter, the impacts of monetary and fiscal policies on macroeconomic variables were examined under fixed and flexible exchange rates, based on the assumption that the underlying macroeconomic structure of the economy was as specified in equations (6.2) to (6.10). No disaggregation of domestic output was attempted; so no sectoral issues were discussed. It was simply assumed that domestic output (or, in the limiting case, the price level) responded positively to increases in desired expenditure levels. In this chapter, attention is given to the differences that arise when the underlying macroeconomic structure of the economy differs significantly from that assumed in Chapter 6.

Given the ferment in macroeconomic theory at the present time, such explorations are necessarily tentative, and this chapter is meant only to provide the reader with a preliminary introduction to such classes of models and their effects on analyses of exchange-rate systems and policy alternatives. Given the relative newness of the macroeconomic ideas themselves, it is hardly surprising that analysis of their properties in conjunction with exchange-rate questions has only begun.

150

Two major types of macroeconomic structures significantly different from that assumed in Chapter 6 can be distinguished. In one, the assumption that markets clear in the short run can be abandoned. The effects, in general, of that abandonment on the analysis of the effects of exchange rate and domestic policies are the subject of Section 7.1. A special case of non-market-clearing is rigidity in the real wage, for one reason or another. An analysis of that situation is presented in Section 7.2. Finally, the sectoral issues of macroeconomic policy arising from large shifts in the terms of trade are considered in Section 7.3.

7.1 **Fix-price models**

One type of model developed for a closed economy has been based on the assumption that some prices cannot adjust in the short run, but that not all market participants can carry out the transactions they wish to at prevailing prices. When that happens, quantities must adjust, and the volume of transactions is the lesser of demand and supply. Simultaneously, there is rationing of that quantity (by some arbitrarily assumed rule) to the other side of the market, and transactors then recalculate their demands for other goods based on amounts actually obtained in the rationed market. Four types of temporary equilibria have been distinguished under this set of mechanisms: a classical equilibrium in which the real wage is too high and consumers face rationing when buying commodities and when selling labor; a Keynesian unemployment equilibrium in which there is excess supply in both the commodity market and the labor market; a "repressed-inflation" equilibrium in which there is excess demand in both the commodity market and the labor market (and goods and workers are rationed among households and firms); and an "excess-demand" equilibrium in which there is an excess demand for labor and a trade deficit. For present purposes, an important point about these models is that economies switch from one region to another as relative prices change, and the responses of the economy to various disturbances may differ from one region to another.

Dixit (1978) applied this framework to the analysis of changes in the balance of trade and the exchange rate. He used a one-commodity model with labor and money, but no other assets, for a small country in short-run equilibrium, with given money supply, wage rate, and price level. By assumption of a small country, commodities are freely tradable, so that any differences between output and demand are reflected in a trade imbalance.

Rationing in the Dixit model therefore can occur only in the labor market, and there are two different regions for policy, depending on whether the market is in surplus (i.e., consumers are rationed in how much labor they can sell) or in deficit (i.e., there is an excess demand for labor, and firms cannot buy as much as they would like in the short run). There is also a region of trade-balance surplus and one of deficit. Exchange-rate policy in the Dixit model reduces to a choice of domestic price level, because the price of the single good is assumed fixed in foreign currency. Monetary and fiscal policies can be thought of as shifting temporary equilibrium points, as shown in Figure 7.1.

The curve *FE* corresponds to points of zero excess demand for labor; all points above it (i.e., with a higher real wage) correspond to points of excess labor supply, and all points below it correspond to excess demand for labor. The *BT* line represents points at which the demand for goods is equal to output. Its slope can be ambiguous, because

> a higher wage leads to a greater demand for output, but by increasing the labour supply it relaxes the constraint on the producers, so it also gives a higher supply of output . . . If the elasticity of labour supply is small and the income effect on consumption is large, $\partial s/\partial w$ [the partial response of the excess supply of goods to a change in the nominal wage] has a good chance of being negative [Dixit, 1978, pp. 396–7].

The slope of *BT* is likely to change at the point where the economy shifts from labor rationing to unemployment, and it

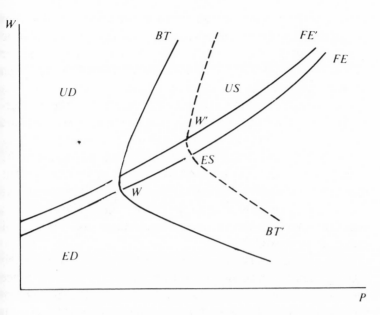

Figure 7.1. Regions of temporary equilibrium and effects of a shift. *U*, excess supply of labor; *E*, excess demand for labor; *S*, trade surplus; *D*, trade deficit.

may change sign. As shown in Figure 7.1, the *BT* line, or zero-balance-of-trade line, is discontinuous at *FE* and shifts from negative to positive slope. There is trade surplus to the right of the *BT* line and trade deficit to the left, as indicated.

In response to an expansion in the money supply, the economy will move in the long run from the initial equilibrium point *W* to the new equilibrium point *W*", as *BT* and *FE* shift to *BT'* and *FE'*. However, in the short run, wages and prices are sticky, and the economy will remain at *W,* which has become a point of excess demand for labor and trade deficit. If prices and wages do not adjust over time, a price-specie-flow mechanism will gradually reduce the money supply and drive the economy back to the original equilibrium at *W* (with the *BT* and *FE* curves gradually shifting back to their original levels). If money wages can gradually adjust, the economy will move up vertically from *W*, meeting the labor-market-equilibrium locus (which will be below *FE'* because trade-balance deficits will have reduced the money supply somewhat), and then drift downward again as trade-balance deficits persist.

If, finally, the exchange rate can adjust initially (the flexible-exchange-rate case?) to the new equilibrium level while wages are sticky, the economy will move to the right immediately to the *BT'* curve and then move gradually along *BT'* to meet *W''*, with the money supply remaining constant at its new, higher level. In the case of monetary contraction, the short run corresponds to Keynesian underemployment equilibrium (with a trade surplus), and the adjustment mechanism is the reverse of that following expansion.

With expansionary fiscal policy, the *BT* curve shifts to the right, but there is no change in the labor market. This is because the government's additional expenditures are on the single commodity and are met by additional imports (reduced exports). Hence, expansionary fiscal policy results in a trade-balance deficit, and nothing else. This result hinges on the assumption of sticky prices and wages and is tantamount to assuming a fixed exchange rate for a small open economy in which all goods are traded: Fiscal policy is powerless to affect the level of economic activity.

Cuddington (1980) recently extended this sort of fix-price model by disaggregating it to allow for an exportable good in less than perfectly elastic demand, but with short-run fix price and an importable good for which it is assumed that the world price is always given. He assumed that when there is excess demand for the exportable good, it is rationed, so that domestic demand is satisfied first, and whatever remains is exported.[1]

---

[1] There is also a labor-rationing rule for the repressed-inflation case. Under this rule, an increase in the price level increases labor supply, whereas an increase in the price of either commodity alone causes reallocation of labor with a constant total supply. Cuddington noted that the results of his model are sensitive to the assumptions made with regard to the rationing rule.

There is an interesting question as to the meaning of perfectly elastic world demand with domestic fix price that is invariant with respect to exchange-rate changes.

In the case of classical unemployment (with excess demand for goods), Cuddington found that government expenditures have no effect on the level of output or employment. If the government increases its expenditure on the exportable (given that its price is constant), the amount available for export merely decreases, and the worsening of the trade balance is the only effect. Government expenditures on importables simply increase the quantity of goods imported.

Given that the price of exports is fixed in the short run, even with exchange-rate changes, then exports decrease, and the change in import volume is ambiguous, but the trade balance necessarily improves in response to devaluation. It should be recalled that, by assumption, the initial situation was one in which there was unsatisfied excess demand for exports, which accounts for this result. Exchange-rate changes can affect employment and output in the import-competing industry, however, and therefore can affect the overall level of economic activity.

In the Keynesian unemployment case, increased government expenditure on the exportable can stimulate output and employment, but expenditures on the import-competing good are ineffective: In either case, the trade balance deteriorates in response to expansionary fiscal policy. A devaluation can increase both output and employment in both exportable and import-competing sectors. In repressed-inflation situations, policies stimulating aggregate demand have no effect on output and employment, but a currency devaluation can improve the trade balance.

Even though one can question whether or not Cuddington's particular assumptions are economically meaningful, what emerges most strongly from the Cuddington analysis is the indeterminacy of the effects of exchange-rate changes in the short run if the initial situation is one of disequilibrium, unless the nature of the disequilibrium is specified. There are some grounds for hoping that situations of repressed inflation (and excess demand for labor) might be empirically distinguishable from situations of unemployment, either classical or Keynesian. But the distinction between the latter may also be important. This highlights the importance of the assumptions made about the real wage and its role in macroeconomic equilibrium, to which we next turn.[2]

In another direction, Liviatan (1979) examined the Mundell-Fleming results in light of the fix-price rationing model. Letting the price of untraded goods adjust only slowly in response to excess demand, he found that the Mundell-Fleming results still apply, but that the effect of a monetary expansion (under fixed exchange rates) would be to incur a larger balance-of-payments deficit than would be realized with instantaneous price adjustment. This result follows because with excess demand for nontraded goods that cannot be satisfied, consumers spend more on traded goods than they would were their demand for nontraded goods satisfied.

When, instead, rigidity is assumed in the nominal wage rather than in the price of nontraded goods, monetary policy can lead to cycles under fixed exchange rates, because an expansion induces employment increases, whereas contraction of the monetary stock resulting from a trade deficit then leads to unemployment. A sufficient devaluation can prevent the unemployment result, and flexible exchange rates will eliminate the cycling.

7.2 Real-wage-rigidity models

Most earlier macroeconomic models of open economies either ignored the labor market or implicitly or explicitly assumed fixity of the nominal wage. Recently, a number of authors have begun analyzing the behavior of an economy sub-

---

[2] Helpman's two studies (1976, 1977) of a wage restriction and Neary's assumed-wage restriction and sticky price of nontradable goods, which will be covered in Section 7.2, are also fix-price models.

ject to a wage constraint such that increases in prices are accompanied by an instantaneous or lagged response of nominal wages.[3] The response may be partial or total, but in any case, real-wage behavior becomes a parameter of the system and is taken into account in evaluating the impact of exchange-rate changes or of fiscal and monetary policies.

Generally, real-wage-rigidity models assume traded and non-traded goods (see Section 3.2).[4] The price level is then a weighted average of the behavior of home-goods prices and traded-goods prices. Wage indexation takes the form of adjusting the nominal wage in response to changes in either class of prices. Full indexation takes place when the nominal wage rises proportionately with the weighted average of home-goods and traded-goods prices.

The significant point about this formulation is that there is no longer a single aggregate supply function: It is possible for the price of one type of good to change so that the real wage falls in terms of, say, traded goods, while rising in terms of non-traded goods, or conversely. For different weights attached to home goods and traded goods in nominal-wage determination, different output responses are possible, whether indexation is complete or less than complete. In some models, such as that of Bruno (1978), lags in adjusting nominal wages to devaluation

[3] In addition to the models of real-wage rigidity considered here, the "Norwegian" model focuses on the role of the real wage and its place in macroeconomic policy. In the Scandinavian model, however, the assumed mechanism is that the exchange rate and the rate of growth of productivity in traded-goods industries jointly determine the money wage (and real wage in terms of traded goods). That wage is then also the wage in nontraded-goods industries. The implications of the model are much the same as those of the monetary approach to the balance of payments: The exchange rate affects the price level rather than real variables within the economy. See Aukrust (1977) for an exposition.

[4] An exception is Van Wijnbergen (1980), who focused on an oil price shock in the context of a small country producing only one traded good that uses oil as an intermediate input. He contrasted output responses to an oil price increase and a devaluation under flexible and fixed real wages. In all cases, output responses were larger under rigidity.

permit real effects to occur in the short run, but not in the long run after full adjustment. Devaluation and macroeconomic policy have real effects only in the interval between impact and the return to initial real values.

One of the early studies to adopt the indexation assumption was that of Casas (1975). He showed that with full indexation of the wage and perfect capital mobility, the Mundell-Fleming assignments are reversed: Changes in the supply of money do not affect the level of output, whereas fiscal expansion can raise real output. Monetary policy is ineffective because it cannot affect the real wage. Fiscal policy, by contrast, induces a capital inflow such that the exchange rate need not depreciate very much (and might even appreciate). If fiscal policy shifts the demand for nontraded goods upward, while the exchange rate fails to depreciate, the real wage in terms of nontraded goods will decline, and output in that sector will expand.[5]

Sachs (1980) extended the Casas analysis further to cover the case of lagged indexation, a response of wages to sustained unemployment, and wealth effects under assumptions of full capital mobility and perfect foresight. When there is a lag in indexing wages, monetary policy can work in the short run (because the real wage drops temporarily below its pegged level), and short-run fiscal multipliers become smaller than they would otherwise be. In addition, whereas under nominal-wage rigidity an expansion of output increases output in the rest of the world, an output increase induced by fiscal policy under real-wage rigidity reduces output in the rest of the world (because the decline in the real wage induced at home by exchange-rate appreciation is offset by an increase in the real wage abroad).

Modigliani and Padoa-Schioppa (1978) examined the prop-

---

[5] Several important studies have interpreted macroeconomic behavior in the developed countries since 1973 as occurring in the context of fixed real wages in Europe and Japan and nominal-wage rigidity in the United States and Canada. See Branson and Rotemberg (1980), Bruno and Sachs (1979), and Sachs (1979) on this issue.

erties of macroeconomic management under wage indexation in an open economy. They assumed "100% plus" indexation, although permitting lags in the adjustment of nominal wages to nominal prices. In a closed economy, for each real wage there is a noninflationary rate of output (NIRO) that will be lower the higher the wage. If output is raised above that level by demand-management policies, even with unemployment remaining in the system, a process of continuous inflation is set in motion. The rate of inflation is higher the greater the gap between the rate of output sustained by demand management and the NIRO and also the shorter the lags in adjusting wages to price increases.

For an open economy, the situation is not significantly different under flexible exchange rates, although the underlying model is more complicated. There is only one real-wage rate consistent with the ratio of domestic prices to foreign prices such that the current account will balance under conditions of full employment. A higher real wage is consistent with a lower level of output if the current account is to be balanced. Under managed floating, however, there can also be a cycling process. The inflationary process leads to a deterioration of the current account, which tends to reduce income and employment. Pressures to depreciate arise as the rate of inflation accelerates. Restrictive monetary and fiscal policies and a devaluation occur, restoring balance to the current account, but inducing unemployment. The cycling continues, because the continuous rate of inflation is inconsistent with any sustained nominal exchange rate. These authors concluded that fiscal policy is relatively powerless to affect the situation:

> This role [of fiscal policy] is likely to be narrow once other long-run implications of the composition of demand and of foreign indebtedness are taken into account. In general, therefore, fiscal policy cannot be counted upon to contribute much by itself toward a solution of the three-way problem of achieving full employment, price stability, and external equilibrium,

but it can help to make it more manageable for a limited time [Modigliani and Padoa-Schioppa, 1978, p. 35].

Helpman (1977), also using a wage-indexation model in the context of traded and nontraded goods, provided a careful analysis of the impact of policies. The analysis is short-run in nature, and asset effects are ignored. He specified nominal wages as a function of nominal commodity prices:

$$w \geq y(p_n, p_t) \tag{7.1}$$

where w is the economywide nominal wage, p_n is the price of the nontraded good, and p_t is the price of the traded good. Letting w_i be the partial elasticity of the wage function with respect to the price of commodity i, he assumed that $0 \leq w_i \leq 1$, with money illusion if $\Sigma w_i < 1$. The inequality, of course, may also hold in the event that demand for labor, rather than indexation, determines the wage, but that case is ruled out in Helpman's analysis.

Producers, with capital fixed in the short run, maximize profits by varying the quantity of labor employed, which generates labor-demand, L_i, and output-supply, Q_i, functions:

$$L_i = L_{di}(p_i/w) \quad (i = n, t) \tag{7.2}$$
$$Q_i = S_i(p_i/w) \quad (i = n, t) \tag{7.3}$$

The government sector buys commodities G_n (nontraded) and G_t (traded), raises taxes in amount T, and sets the exchange rate R. Demand for nontradables, D_n, must then equal supply of nontradables, S_n, as an equilibrium condition:

$$D_n[p_n, p_t; p_iS_i/(p_i/w) - T] + G_n = S_n(p_n/w) \tag{7.4}$$

That relation, the wage-setting equation, and a condition that sets labor demand equal to labor employment provide a system of three equations in three unknowns. At equilibrium, the deficit in the trade account equals the deficit in the government's budget $(T - \Sigma p_i G_i)$.

From examination of equation (7.4) it is immediately apparent that an increase in government spending on traded commodities cannot affect resource allocation in the domestic economy. The government can, through expenditures, affect the level of economic activity only insofar as the expenditures are on nontraded goods. Because reducing taxes also leads to an increased private demand for nontraded goods, increased government expenditures on nontraded goods are equivalent to (some larger magnitude of) reduced government tax receipts.

When the government increases expenditures on nontraded goods, the resulting excess demand raises the price of nontraded goods and their output. It also induces an increase in the money wage as a consequence of the increase in the price of nontraded goods. If the elasticity of the wage with respect to home goods is less than unity, the outcome will be an increase in output of nontradables and an increase in employment in that sector. However, there will be an offset insofar as, at a fixed exchange rate, employment in tradables will go down because of the higher real wage (denominated in terms of tradables). Total employment may either rise or fall, depending on the relative magnitudes of the traded- and nontraded-goods sectors, the responsiveness of the nominal wages to the price of nontradables, and the elasticity of demand for labor in the traded-goods sector.

A devaluation reduces the real wage in traded-goods industries, thus causing an expansion of output and income, and a consequent increase in the demand for nontradables. If the proportional size of the nontradable sector is larger than the marginal propensity to consume nontraded goods, there will be an increase in the relative price of tradable goods. If, on the other hand, the marginal propensity to consume nontraded goods exceeds the relative size of the nontradable sector, the foreign-currency price of home goods will rise, and a trade-balance deficit will increase as a consequence of devaluation. Devaluation decreases the size of the trade deficit if and only if the relative price of tradable goods rises as a consequence.

In a related article, using much the same underlying model but with capital mobile between sectors, Helpman (1976) extended the analysis in a different direction, a direction also followed by Neary (1980) and Jones and Corden (1976). In both the Helpman study and that of Jones and Corden the key variables are the factor intensities of the traded- and nontraded-goods sectors. In the Helpman model, supplies of each good are perfectly elastic at average cost. If government expenditures raise the demand for nontraded goods, the outcome hinges on factor intensities. If the nontraded-goods sector is labor-intensive, the additional labor demanded can be supplied from the unemployed labor force at the prevailing nominal wage with no change in output prices. However, if the nontraded goods are capital-intensive, the labor released from the traded-goods sector will not be entirely absorbed in the nontraded-goods sector. Consequently, expansionary fiscal policy (expenditures on the nontraded good) can raise income only if the nontraded-goods sector is labor-intensive. If it is capital-intensive, increased demand for nontraded goods increases unemployment, given the wage rigidity of the model.

The results are analogous in the case of a devaluation. Factor prices rise, following devaluation, in terms of local currency. devaluation increases the relative price of tradable commodities if nontradables are labor-intensive and lowers the balance-of-trade deficit. However, if tradables are capital-intensive, devaluation increases the relative price of nontradables and increases the trade-balance deficit.

The Jones-Corden results are similar. Both factors are mobile. If nominal wages are constant (due, perhaps, to that being the target of monetary and fiscal policy), a devaluation raises the return to capital (because the nominal wage does not rise) in the traded-goods sector. If nontradables are relatively more capital-intensive than tradables, their relative price increases, and the trade balance worsens.

Neary dealt instead with the case in which wages and the

price of nontradables are sticky in the short run. In a model that has the long-run properties of a flexible-price model, he analyzed the various regions of temporary quantity-constrained equilibrium that can arise under short-run inflexible wages and nontraded-goods prices. If, when labor is rationed, traded-goods firms receive priority in their labor allocation (and thus are unconstrained), whereas nontraded-goods producers are constrained, three regimes are possible (in addition to full long-run Walrasian equilibrium): classical unemployment, with households rationed in selling their labor and buying nontraded goods; repressed inflation, with households rationed in the nontraded-goods market and firms unable to hire the quantity of labor they demand; and Keynesian unemployment with nontraded-goods firms rationed in the quantity they can sell and households rationed in the quantity of labor they can sell. If nontraded-goods producers receive priority allocation of labor, a fourth regime, with households unconstrained, traded-goods firms rationed in the labor market, and nontraded-goods firms rationed in the goods market, is also possible (under-consumption).

Generally, starting from a Walrasian equilibrium, monetary policy has the expected effects, because an expansion of the money supply leads to the repressed-inflation regime, whereas contractionary monetary policy moves the economy (in the short run) into the Keynesian unemployment regime. Government purchases of traded goods (fiscal policy) are ineffective and simply lead to a deterioration in the balance of trade; government purchases of nontraded goods are effective in increasing employment and output of nontradables, except when the initial equilibrium is one in which there is excess demand for nontradables.

Devaluation expands regions of excess demand for labor and for nontradables. If traded and nontraded goods are gross substitutes, indirect cross-price effects make devaluation even more effective. If not, a devaluation could lead to the underconsumption regime in which each type of firm faces one constraint. The conditions under which devaluation can worsen the trade balance with Keynesian unemployment are opposite to those derived by Helpman (1977) because of the assumed rigidity in the nontraded-goods market. Neary summarized his findings, noting that

> taking all possible regimes together, exchange rate policy was found to exert a more predictable influence on the level of employment than fiscal or monetary policy, whereas the reverse was true of the influence of these two sets of instruments on the trade balance [Neary, 1980, p. 427].

7.3 Sectoral shifts

Readers who recall the literature of the 1950s and 1960s will find it ironic that terms-of-trade effects, so prominent in earlier literature on the effects of exchange-rate changes, had largely disappeared from the discussion by the time that the first OPEC oil price increase had occurred. The fact that the 1970s witnessed the adoption of flexible exchange rates, the oil price increases, and accelerating worldwide inflation accompanied by stagflation or unemployment naturally led to models of the possible effects of terms-of-trade shifts, often for imports of an intermediate good, on the level of domestic economic activity and rate of price increases. Much of the focus was sectoral, contrasting the impacts on particular sectors of an oil price increase (for importers and for exporters) and a mineral discovery or other exogenous increase in wealth.

Corden (1977, Chapters 7 and 8) summarized the standard approach to the impact of the oil price increase: It redistributed income from the rest of the world to OPEC, to producers of oil substitutes from others, and to producers of goods for which OPEC had a relatively high marginal propensity to consume. The first effect obviously dominated, and to the extent that oil exporters had a higher marginal propensity to save than oil importers, there was required a world increase in real investment and a decrease in the real rate of interest.[6]

If the real rate of interest and the nominal wage were constant in the short run, the net effect would be (under conventional Keynesian assumptions) a decline in aggregate demand and an increase in the price level. If there is monetary accommodation, the deflationary effects can be mitigated, but at the cost of even larger increases in the price level.

The impact effect, at constant real exchange rate and money wage, would be current-account deficits for oil importers, which Corden termed the "full-employment oil deficit." To the extent that some countries chose more deflationary policies relative to others, those countries then tended to experience partially offsetting current-account surpluses. Flexible exchange rates served to keep real exchange rates relatively constant among oil importers, thereby preventing still other effects that might have resulted from differential rates of price increases in response to the oil price rise.

Several attempts have been made to extend the analysis in a variety of directions. Bruno's model (1978), cited earlier, is perhaps representative of many in the group, where an increase in the price of an importable good leads to unemployment and excess supply in the short run, as nominal-wage rigidity prevents the downward adjustment in the real wage necessitated by an increase in the price of an importable intermediate good.

An early treatment of the role of imported intermediate inputs, and price changes for them, was undertaken by Findlay and Rodriguez (1977) in the context of a modified Mundell-

---

[6] The required increase in world investment is not the same as the "recycling" problem. Immediately after the first large oil price increase, policymakers were concerned that OPEC would not spend its export earnings and that the developed countries would experience balance-of-payments difficulties. This concern was based on a fundamental confusion: To the extent that OPEC did not spend its proceeds, it automatically accumulated foreign exchange or other assets.

Fleming model.[7] They assumed a flexible exchange rate under which a single domestic good is produced with labor, capital, and an intermediate good. Capital is fixed in the short run.[8] They assumed a perfectly elastic supply of capital from abroad (as did Mundell and Fleming) so that they could infer the signs of changes in the current account and assume that offsetting capital flows are forthcoming under flexible exchange rates. The money-demand function is conventional, because real balances are assumed to depend on the (fixed) world rate of interest and real income. The assumption of a unitary income elasticity of demand permits simplification.

For given nominal exchange rate and wage, there will be equilibrium values of the domestic price level and real exchange rate (the nominal exchange rate divided by the price of domestic output), derived from a goods-equilibrium condition (where a higher domestic price level must be offset by a higher real exchange rate) and a money-market-equilibrium condition (also upward-sloping, but less steeply).

In this setup, Findlay and Rodriguez found that, holding the domestic price level and the real exchange rate constant, an increase in the price of an imported intermediate input will lead to an excess demand for money and either an excess demand for or an excess supply of the domestic good: Output of the domestic good clearly falls, but demand may decline even more

[7] Findlay has also modeled the reaction function of an oil cartel and oil importers (whose level of output is a function of the quantity of oil imported under sticky nominal wages). He found output decreasing in importing countries in response to reduced supplies, and he found the optimal supply (from the cartel's viewpoint) falling in response to lowered output.

[8] Findlay and Rodriguez asserted that they assumed fixed coefficients between output and the intermediate good in production. In fact, there are points in their analysis at which they implicitly assumed substitutability between the intermediate good and labor (e.g., when they concluded that it is possible for output to increase while employment falls). It does not appear that their analysis is invalidated by this.

if there are increased expenditures on the imported intermediate good (i.e., a total elasticity of demand for it of less than unity). Whether an increased price of an imported intermediate good is on impact inflationary or deflationary depends on whether demand or supply of the home good declines more.[9] When markets clear, however, the domestic price level must increase in consequence of an increased intermediate-good price,[10] whereas the exchange rate can go in either direction.

Monetary policy works in much the same way as in the Mundell-Fleming model: Expansionary monetary policy raises the domestic price level, thereby lowering the real wage and increasing output. Simultaneously, the real exchange rate depreciates, thus increasing the cost of the imported intermediate input, but the net effect is to increase output. As Findlay and Rodriguez explained,

> while increases in the nominal money supply and in government expenditure both increase real output, they do so in opposite ways. Expansionary monetary policy achieves its effects by increasing the domestic price level and thus cheapening the real cost of labour, which more than offsets the contractionary impact of the depreciation of the real exchange rate that makes the imported intermediate input more expensive . . . Expansionary monetary policy always increases employment since output can only increase in spite of higher real cost of the intermediate input if employment increases. The opposite effects on the real exchange rate mean that expansionary monetary policy improves the trade balance while expansionary fis-

---

[9] The inflation is defined in terms of the price of the domestically produced good. If an index were formed including the intermediate import, a decreased price of the final domestic good would not be sufficient.

[10] This price increase must take place to restore monetary equilibrium, because the unchanged stock of money will not willingly be held with reduced output and price level.

cal policy worsens it [Findlay and Rodriguez, 1977, pp. 215–16].

If the real wage, rather than the nominal wage, is fixed, real output can be influenced only by the real exchange rate. There is only one real exchange rate at which the goods market clears; monetary policy becomes ineffective because it cannot affect the real exchange rate, whereas fiscal policy can affect the real exchange rate and thus induce increased output and employment (by cheapening the imported intermediate good). Thus, in the Findlay-Rodriguez model, fiscal policy can affect the level of economic activity by altering the relative price of an input in terms of the output through affecting the real exchange rate.

Obstfeld (1980*b*) extended the Findlay-Rodriguez analysis to incorporate the effects of intertemporal utility maximization on behavior in the face of an increased price of an imported intermediate good. The Corden expectations with regard to the trade balance and exchange rate are reversed. Prices are fully flexible in his model, and there are two final consumer goods, one domestic and one imported, that yield utility. The foreign price of the imported consumer good and the foreign price of the intermediate import are both given to the country in question. Defining the terms of trade as the ratio of the price of the imported consumer good to the price of the domestically produced consumer good (and leaving out of account the price of the intermediate good), Obstfeld traced the effects of an intermediate-good price increase on the terms of trade, finding that they are likely to improve.[11] Essentially, an increase in the price of the intermediate good lowers the real wage and instantaneous utility. To reattain an optimum, domestic consumers acquire larger income streams from abroad by buying foreign bonds. Hence, the current account is likely to improve for the country

[11] Obstfeld's model obviously does not hold in a three-country world with one oil exporter and one producer for each of the two consumer goods, because the terms of trade cannot improve for both oil importers.

whose imported-intermediate-good price has increased.[12] Obstfeld concluded that

> the results show how partial-equilibrium arguments based on balance-of-payments flow considerations can mislead. When the price-elasticity of demand for intermediates is near zero, a surplus on current account, not a deficit, is almost certain to arise ... Only when there is a significant degree of substitution between imported materials and domestically-available factors and between finished imports and exports is it possible for a current deficit and spot depreciation to occur simultaneously in response to a materials price shock [Obstfeld, 1980*b*, p. 478].

Corden and Neary (1980) focused on the relative price implications of a mineral discovery: the so-called Dutch-disease problem. "The Dutch disease" is the term used to refer to economies wherein there are simultaneously booming and lagging traded-goods industries or sectors. This can involve either the discovery of new (mineral) wealth or an increased price of one exportable leading to an appreciation of the real exchange rate and thus lowering the relative prices of other tradables.

Ironically, just as many industrial countries were blaming their stagflationary economies on the oil price increase of 1973–4 (and later 1979–80), a number of countries were apparently experiencing similar macroeconomic phenomena despite the presence of oil exports or mineral discoveries that left them with improved terms of trade or real-income prospects: Norway, Australia, The Netherlands, and possibly the United Kingdom fell into that category.

Corden and Neary analyzed the booming-sector phenomenon in the context of a model of a small open economy producing

---

[12] Note again the partial-equilibrium nature of the analysis in that the behavior of the oil exporter is only implicit: The exporter must incur current-account deficits, running down his stock of other assets.

two traded goods, manufacturing and other tradables (whose prices are exogenously determined in the world market), and a class of nontraded goods (services). Trade is always balanced, and the effect of a mineral or resource discovery is analyzed as an exogenous Hicks-neutral technical improvement in the non-manufacturing traded-goods sector. It should be noted that such a change is not synonymous with an increase in the world price of the commodity in question, a consideration to which we shall turn later (see the discussion of the contribution of Buiter and Purvis). The analysis is essentially short-run in nature, with the capital stock of each of the three sectors assumed to be immobile, whereas labor is assumed mobile between sectors.

In the Corden-Neary model, it is clear that in response to the "technical improvement," the total output of traded goods must increase, but output of nontraded goods may rise or fall, and manufacturing output must fall. Thus, output of the mineral increases by more than output of manufactures falls. The change in the wage rate relative to the price of services is indeterminate, so that a sufficiently large increase in the price of services could lead to a decrease in the real wage. If manufacturing is capital-intensive relative to nontraded goods, the profitability of the manufacturing sector may increase (as increases in the wage rate reduce profitability in the more labor-intensive sectors).

Assuming that desired money stocks are in fixed proportion to nominal income and that the private sector hoards or dishoards to attain its desired level of money balances, a boom decreases the nominal price level (with constant money supply). Under fixed exchange rates, the initial adjustment in the price of services is less than the long-run adjustment; a balance-of-payments surplus tends to increase the money supply over time, thus increasing the price of nontraded goods until the new equilibrium is reached. If the Central Bank sterilizes the surplus, the relative price of traded goods remains higher than it would be at full equilibrium, and the traded-goods sector (both booming and manufacturing components) is "protected." The "deindustrialization" process is less severe and less prolonged than it would otherwise be.

By contrast, a floating exchange rate lets the new long-run-equilibrium relative price of nontraded goods be attained instantaneously (with an appreciation of the exchange rate), although this may require a decrease in the nominal wage. If the nominal wage were sticky, unemployment could result. Thus, in the Corden-Neary model, a resource discovery can lead not only to a decline in the relative and absolute importance of the manufacturing traded-goods sector but also to prolonged unemployment under floating exchange rates if the monetary authorities fail to permit domestic inflation to adjust the level of real wages.

Buiter and Purvis (1980) provided an analysis of the differences between monetary disinflation, an oil price increase (for an oil exporter, as well as for an importer), and a discovery of oil in the context of a Dornbusch (1976) overshooting model with sluggish adjustment in the goods market and perfect foresight. They did not consider the role of oil as an intermediate good, focusing instead on the "demand" shock aspects of an unanticipated change in monetary growth, an unanticipated oil discovery, and an unanticipated permanent increase in the price of oil on the time path of the real exchange rate. In the case of an unanticipated permanent reduction in the rate of money-supply growth (equal to the anticipated rate of inflation), there are no long-run effects on the real exchange rate, but, as in the Dornbusch model (1976), there is exchange-rate overshooting in the short run because asset markets adjust faster than goods markets to the increased demand for real balances.

An oil price increase generates different effects on permanent real income, depending on whether a country is a net exporter or a net importer. In the case in which it is a net exporter, the long-run real exchange rate must appreciate; in the short run, it can either appreciate (with or without overshooting) or depreciate (overshooting), depending on whether the output of the domestically produced nontraded good is more responsive to the foreign price of oil or to the real exchange rate. When the real exchange rate appreciates with initial overshooting (i.e., it appreciates more than the long-run amount and then depreciates to reach the steady state), Dutch disease and a decline in the output of the domestically produced non-oil good can result. For a net oil importer, an increase in the price of oil generates a long-run real depreciation (although the impact effect on the real exchange rate can be positive or negative) of the exchange rate. While the real exchange rate is below its long-run equilibrium, there is a loss in output of the non-oil good because its relative price is below that prevailing in the long run.

Buiter and Purvis complicated the analysis of an oil discovery by assuming that it gives rise to (correct) expectations that oil output will be positive for a finite period of time. They thus treated it as a combination of two disturbances: a permanent unanticipated immediate increase in oil output and an anticipated permanent decline in oil output at some future date. The effect is for instantaneous appreciation of the real exchange rate, overshooting its long-run equilibrium, followed by gradual depreciation. During the period of oil production, the current account is in surplus, and the currency is depreciating, because transitory income is above permanent income. This is the Dutch-disease case.

Natural-resource discoveries and exogenous increases in the price of oil are essentially increases in wealth, and they may also have relative price effects. Analysis of their effects depends crucially on assumptions about expectations, price flexibility, intertemporal maximization, and probably also factor-substitution possibilities (when the role as an intermediate input is taken into account). Any model incorporating the possible combinations and permutations of all these features would undoubtedly be hopelessly complex and unmanageable. Nonetheless, there appears to be considerable scope for simplifying the analysis and incorporating it more closely with the type of intertemporal models discussed in Chapter 5.

8

Payments regimes and developing countries

As mentioned in Chapter 6, analysis of "adjustment mechanisms" traditionally begins with the proposition that there are essentially three means by which a country's external accounts may be kept in balance: monetary and fiscal policies under fixed exchange rates responding to the imperatives of the balance of payments; flexible exchange rates; and exchange control, under which quantitative restrictions on international transactions are adjusted to restrict payments to foreigners to a level commensurate with foreign-exchange availability from earnings and borrowing.

The preceding chapters have been concerned largely with situations in which either fixed or flexible exchange rates have been the chief mechanism used. This does not imply that countries adopting one or the other of these regimes have not employed any quantitative restrictions, but rather that any such restrictions have been imposed for motives other than balance-of-payments constraints and have been relatively invariant with respect to the availability of foreign exchange. To be sure, almost all countries have imposed some controls on capital transactions, and, as already seen, the relaxation of those controls has been a key aspect of the evolution of international trade and the increasing importance of capital since the end of World War II. Among the developed countries, there is now virtually unrestricted convertibility on both current account and capital account, and the key question facing the international economy pertains to the development of international arrangements to maintain and facilitate the largely integrated trade and payments network.

By contrast, most developing countries have adopted restrictionist trade and payments regimes over much of the postwar period. Quantitative restrictions have been employed on current account, and there have been virtually prohibitive restrictions on capital outflows, while the fact of nonconvertibility has largely precluded inward mobility of capital.

A first question is the extent to which the analysis of the preceding chapters applies to exchange-control regimes. That is the subject of Section 8.1. It will be seen that although there are some similar components, there are also some special features of exchange-control regimes that warrant different analysis. One such feature is the emergence of a black market. That phenomenon will be discussed in Section 8.2. A related feature involves the questions that arise with regard to the estimation of an equilibrium exchange rate and the use of a crawling peg, which will be covered in Section 8.3. Section 8.4 will then treat the very difficult problems confronting policymakers in countries with highly restrictionist regimes who wish to alter their trade and payments regimes.

8.1 **Analysis of exchange-control regimes**

Assume that a small country, unable to affect its terms of trade, is in full equilibrium at a fixed exchange rate in a constant-price-level world. It then begins to increase the domestic-credit component of the monetary base at a rate of x percent. Under fixed exchange rates with full convertibility, the payments situation will shift, as domestic residents trade excess domestic money for foreign goods and assets. At the fixed exchange rate, continuous domestic-credit creation will be accompanied by a continuous deficit, at least as long as the country can run down its international reserves.

Suppose instead that the domestic monetary authority, while still creating credit, imposes exchange control, so that all foreign-exchange receipts must be surrendered to the government, and the government then auctions off those receipts to the highest bidders. Under usual monetary assumptions, the domestic price level will increase at approximately the rate of growth of domestic credit. However, because the world price of the exportable is given, and the exchange rate is by hypothesis fixed, the domestic price of importables, cut off from the link to the world price via exchange restrictions, will rise. Thus, the domestic price of exportables relative to import-competing goods will fall over time, even at a fixed exchange rate.

As this simple example illustrates, several features of an exchange-control regime are quite distinct from a convertible-currency regime: (1) The nominal exchange rate matters, because it determines the degree to which the relative price of import-competing goods exceeds their world relative price. (2) An exchange-control regime is obviously nonoptimal from the resource-allocation viewpoint. (3) A devaluation of the currency will tend to raise the domestic price of the exportable and leave the domestic price of the import-competing good unaffected if the quantity rationed is not reduced.[1] Devaluation thus affects the domestic relative prices of the various classes of tradable commodities.[2] In addition, it is quite possible that the authorities will allocate import licenses on a quantity basis, giving rise to a premium received by licensees. In such cases, the manner in which licenses are allocated, and the presence of the premiums on import licenses, can have resource-allocation effects as well as income-distribution effects (see Bhagwati, 1978, for a full discussion).[3]

---

[1] For an analysis of the real effects and resource pulls of devaluation with exchange control, see Dervis (1980).

[2] Sohmen (1958) first noted that if imports increased with devaluation; the net effect might even be a decline in the price level, with exportable prices rising and importable prices falling.

[3] There are other differences, as well, but they are not central to analysis of the payments regime. See Krueger (1978, Chapter 5).

Because of these effects, it is much more difficult to distinguish the monetary analysis from the real analysis of exchange-control regimes than with fixed- or flexible-exchange-rate regimes. The instruments that are used to contain excess demand for foreign exchange have both monetary and real consequences. One can no longer aggregate importable and exportable commodities into a single category of tradable goods, even though the international price may be given; hence, the relative price of nontradables as a concept itself becomes ambiguous, and even the definition of a real exchange rate becomes troublesome.

Conceptually, analysis of exchange-rate changes may be thought of as consisting of two components: one aimed at correcting an existing or anticipated payments imbalance and the other aimed at increasing the relative domestic price of exportables compared with import-competing goods. The former can be analyzed along conventional lines, whereas the latter requires consideration of the change in relative prices between classes of tradables and the extent to which premiums on import licenses, and licensing mechanisms themselves, are eliminated or reduced in importance.

As this discussion suggests, the fix-price models discussed in Section 7.1 would appear to offer a promising line of analysis. To date, only one such model has appeared, that of Cuddington (1981). He assumed that import quotas are set by the government, permitting domestic prices of importable goods above world levels. He also assumed that the domestic price of the importable is constrained by the government below its market-clearing level, even given the restricted level of imports. Two export regimes are distinguished: In one case the country is assumed to be small and subject to a fixed foreign price at which producers may sell all they wish; in the other, export production is limited to a quantity below what producers would choose were they not restricted.

There are two main types of temporary equilibrium: Keynesian and classical. Under both, devaluation always stimulates exportable production and exports. In a classical unemployment situation, devaluation necessarily improves the trade balance, which need not be the case with Keynesian underemployment in the case of less than perfectly elastic demand for exports. Relaxation of import quotas reduces exportable production and exports in the Keynesian unemployment case, but leaves them unaffected with classical unemployment, with the effect on the balance of trade (measured in foreign currency) unequivocally negative for Keynesian unemployment and ambiguously signed for classical unemployment. Thus, the most important result of the analysis is the finding that the effects of particular policies may differ depending on the types of temporary-equilibrium levels in developing countries. Under classical unemployment, policy effects may be quite different than those that will prevail under Keynesian unemployment.[4]

Aizenman (1981) modeled a three-good economy (exportable, importable, and nontraded good) in which the importable is subject to a quota in the context of a monetary economy. Import licenses are auctioned, with the proceeds redistributed in a lump-sum fashion. He assumed that the monetary authority pegs the exchange rate, but that currency convertibility permits individuals to adjust their real balances through the balance-of-payments mechanism, thus wedding the monetary approach to the balance of payments to the exchange-control model. Assuming gross substitutability, he found that devaluation from a position in which the quota is binding induces lower relative prices for both the nontraded good and the good subject to quota. As contrasted with a tariff, a quota leads to a larger reduction in the relative price of nontradables following deval-

---

[4] Earlier analyses of developing countries were, in a sense, an extreme version of a fix-price model. The two-gap model, developed by Bruno and Chenery (1962) and Chenery and Strout (1966), essentially treated foreign-exchange earnings as exogenous, while simultaneously positing a fixed-coefficients relationship between imports and domestic output or investment. Either way, focus was on a "foreign-exchange constraint" as a binding factor in economic growth. For developing countries adhering to fixed exchange rates under exchange control, the fact that no prices are permitted to adjust may make the assumptions realistic.

uation and reduces the speed of adjustment of the economy to the new long-run equilibrium following devaluation. He put the point neatly:

> Under a tariff the price of the good protected by it is determined by the world supply (for a given tariff), while under a quota it is determined by the domestic excess demand (assuming the constraint is binding). As a result, any change in domestic excess demand will affect quantities imported under a tariff, and domestic prices under a quota [Aizenman, 1981, p. 12].

A number of authors have noted that devaluation will have a different macroeconomic impact under exchange control than it will have with currency convertibility. It is much more likely to have a net deflationary, or contractionary, impact. Cooper (1971) pointed out that particularly when the initial position is one of a large current-account deficit (perhaps financed by capital inflows or by foreign aid), the increase in nominal income to exporters due to devaluation falls short of the increase in nominal expenditures that would be required to maintain the initial level of real absorption. Hence, the impact effect of devaluation is likely to be deflationary. This effect may be reflected in, or further intensified by, a net decrease in the government budget deficit, as receipts from export taxes and tariffs are likely to increase following devaluation.

Krugman and Taylor (1978) combined Cooper's analysis with Diaz-Alejandro's argument (1963) that there can be strong redistributive effects of devaluation from import-competing interests to export interests to model several deflationary impacts of devaluation within the context of a Keynes-Kalecki growth model.[5]

---

[5] On a related issue, Bruno (1979) argued that devaluation might be deflationary in the context of credit rationing within a semiindustrialized economy. Arguing that with credit rationing, contractionary monetary policy first raises firms' costs and only later affects demand, he showed that reducing the trade deficit may feed through to monetary contraction and hence may be deflationary.

8.2 Analysis of black markets

It has long been recognized that black markets are an accompaniment of most exchange-control regimes. The precise nature of the regime may influence the relationship of the black market to the official exchange rate. In regimes in which tourists' acquisition of foreign exchange is fairly easy, the presence of a relatively low cost means of obtaining foreign exchange may imply a small black-market differential (for notes and bills) even if the regime is highly restrictive for large transactions in which currency is not an economic means of payment. Likewise, the presence of a relatively open border may permit sufficient unrecorded transactions to take place to make the black-market rate much closer than the official rate to "the" operational exchange rate. Clearly, the degree of enforcement of exchange restrictions and the mechanisms under which imports are permitted are also important.

Sheikh (1976) modeled the foreign-exchange market as a function of controls in that market, noting that a tariff as the only intervention creates incentives for smuggling but not for a black-market exchange rate. He assumed that the government retains a pegged exchange rate at which there is excess demand for foreign currency, that it bans all capital outflows, and that it allocates foreign exchange among demanders for current-account transactions. The unsatisfied demand for foreign exchange for capital-outflow purposes then becomes shifted to the black market (and its quantity is independent of the exchange rate). The supply of foreign exchange to the official market becomes a function of the black-market exchange rate, whereas the supply of foreign exchange to the black market is a function of the black-market rate, the degree of risk associated with black-market transactions, and the extent of overinvoicing in the official market.

Under Sheikh's assumptions concerning the allocation of rationed official foreign exchange, the equilibrium black-market rate will be the equilibrium exchange rate associated with no exchange control in the absence of risks in black-market dealings. Because there are risks, the black-market exchange rate is always higher than the equilibrium exchange rate as long as risk operates to decrease demand in the black market by pro- portionately no more than supply (contrasted with the riskless situation).

In conformity with the evolution of focus toward the capital account, other recent research has shifted away from viewing the black-market exchange rate as determined in the current account and instead has used an asset approach. Blejer (1978) analyzed the workings of the black market as determined by monetary variables.[6] In his model, the (flow) supply of foreign exchange to the black market is a function of the ratio of the black-market exchange rate to the official exchange rate, whereas (flow) demand is a function of the variables usually associated with the monetary approach to the balance of pay- ments: the expected rate of return on holding foreign-currency- denominated assets (a function of the foreign interest rate and the expected rate of depreciation of the black-market exchange rate) contrasted with the return on domestic assets, a function of the domestic interest rate and the rate of inflation. The gov- ernment is assumed to alter the official exchange rate in accor- dance with its preference function, itself a function of the dis- parity between the official rate and the black-market exchange rate.

Given these assumptions, the black-market exchange rate behaves very similarly to a freely floating exchange rate; its rate of depreciation is a function of the degree of domestic monetary disequilibrium and the world rate of inflation:

> The black-market exchange rate will depreciate faster the higher the rate of domestic credit expansion rela- tive to the increases in the demand for domestic real cash balances and it will depreciate more slowly the higher is the world rate of inflation [Blejer, 1978, p. 123].

---

[6] Blejer (1978) cited a contemporaneous paper by Fishelson (1976) using the monetary approach to analyze the Israeli black market.

The black-market rate can be constant over time only if domestic monetary expansion proceeds at a rate that gives the same rate of domestic inflation as occurs in the rest of the world.

De Macedo (1980) developed a model of black-market exchange rates using Kouri's model of current-account/capital-account interaction described in Section 5.1 and assuming that the official exchange rate is used for (not necessarily all) current-account transactions and that the private sector's foreign-asset accumulation and decumulation occur only through the black market.[7] The supply of foreign exchange to the black market originates from exporters who underinvoice exports in response to the premium they can obtain in the black market. Importers buy black-market foreign exchange insofar as the tariff is less than the black-market premium. The official exchange rate affects the reported current account more strongly than does the black-market rate, whereas the converse holds for the unreported current account. Implicitly, de Macedo assumed that individuals are free to carry out desired current-account transactions within the exchange-control regime, so that official current-account deficits have their counterpart in black-market sales of foreign assets. To be sure, the official and black-market exchange rates affect the desired portfolio composition.

In de Macedo's model, the results are much the same as those of Kouri: The current-account deficit equals private reduction in foreign assets, and conversely. Long-run equilibrium obtains when desired and actual private holdings of foreign assets are equal at an exchange rate that balances the current account.[8] An increase in the expected rate of depreciation of the black-

---

[7] In a sense, de Macedo's model is a model of a dual exchange market, in which the current- and capital-account transactions are carried out at different exchange rates. The novelty arises in the assumed linkages between the two markets. For earlier analyses of dual exchange markets, see Fleming (1971) and Swoboda (1974).

[8] Net (public plus private) wealth accumulation implicitly occurs only to the extent that underinvoicing of exports occurs. To the extent that there is an official current-account deficit, official holdings of foreign assets decline to offset the increased private holdings.

market exchange rate causes the official current-account deficit to increase and causes a shift from official reserves to private holdings of foreign assets. An unanticipated devaluation, by contrast, reduces desired private holdings of foreign assets by reducing the black-market premium. It succeeds by reducing the desired fraction of wealth individuals wish to hold in foreign assets.

8.3 Equilibrium exchange rates

The facts that individuals are not permitted legally to carry out all their desired transactions and that inflation rates have substantially exceeded the world rate in some exchange-control countries have given rise to two interrelated lines of inquiry. On one hand, there has been a search for a means of estimating "the" equilibrium exchange rate for purposes both of shadow pricing and, occasionally, of estimating the magnitude by which policymakers might alter the exchange rate. On the other hand, policymakers have on occasion adopted a crawling-peg system, under which exchange control is maintained, but the exchange rate is altered periodically by small amounts in order to maintain the price-level differential between the country and the rest of the world constant.

Economists have long sought to find criteria with which to identify "the" equilibrium exchange rate.[9] Tools such as PPP (see Sections 2.2.6 and 4.1.1) have been invoked, and consideration has been given to questions such as the relationship between the black-market exchange rate and the official rate, as discussed in Section 8.2. In the absence of any agreement as to the variables that enter into determination of the real exchange rate (in addition to PPP) under a convertible currency, it is hardly surprising that economists have been unable to answer the question of how that function is affected by the presence of exchange controls. Indeed, what may be surprising is that so much effort has been devoted to the undertaking.

[9] See, in particular, Bacha and Taylor (1971) and the references cited therein.

Aside from noting that there is no generally accepted correct means of estimating the equilibrium exchange rate theoretically or empirically from a position of exchange control (or in response to any other nonmonetary shift in the economy such as the discovery of North Sea oil),[10] two strands of thought should be mentioned. The first is the relationship between the concept of an equilibrium real exchange rate, the shadow-pricing literature, and terms-of-trade changes. The second is the analysis of crawling-peg regimes.

8.3.1 *Equilibrium rates and shadow prices*

Because exchange-control regimes are, by definition, regimes in which there is excess demand for foreign exchange, the social-opportunity cost of foreign exchange diverges from the official price. In many developing countries, the mispricing of foreign exchange has frequently been identified as a major distortion (if not the major distortion) in the pricing mechanism. For cost–benefit analysis, derivation of a shadow price of foreign exchange has been a major challenge.

The literature addressing that challenge is in itself huge and cannot be surveyed here.[11] All that needs to be noted is that, conceptually, the shadow price of foreign exchange that should be used for evaluating projects bears little relationship to the notion of an equilibrium exchange rate that would prevail in the absence of exchange control. Generally, estimating a shadow price of foreign exchange, given exchange control, entails a second-best situation: How does one maximize subject to other distortions within the economy? In addition, questions arise as to when the use of shadow prices is appropriate if the private sector is simultaneously optimizing subject to market prices (and perhaps rationing constraints). Obviously, the question what the

---

[10] Most observers would agree, however, that in the absence of any other identifiable and fairly large shifts, the exchange rate probably is more overvalued by x percent this year than last if the country's inflation rate exceeds the world inflation rate between this year and last by x percent.

[11] The interested reader can see Blitzer, Dasgupta, and Stiglitz (1981) and the references cited therein.

shadow price of foreign exchange may be for project evaluation within the context of foreign-exchange constraints is not the same as the question what the price of foreign exchange would be in a liberalized market.

Turning to the question of the equilibrium rate, in the sense of an exchange rate that would clear the market were exchange controls removed, there are numerous difficulties. There is, first of all, the question what the real exchange rate might be at a given time and then the question of its behavior over time.

For its analysis at a given time, the first fundamental question is how a market-determined exchange rate alters with the imposition (or removal) of, say, an ad valorem tariff on imports. As was seen in earlier chapters, the answer to this question depends on the model used, and there is no consensus. The monetary-approach model of Mussa suggests that the exchange rate will depreciate with the imposition of a tariff and appreciate with its removal (because the tariff changes the price level and so alters the demand for nominal balances). The Helpman-Razin intertemporal maximizing model implies that anything can happen to the equilibrium real exchange rate in response to a tariff change.

The same sorts of questions apply with regard to the behavior of the terms of trade. As was seen in Section 7.3, there is no general agreement as to the relationship between resource discoveries or terms-of-trade changes and the behavior of the real exchange rate. For developing countries subject to terms-of-trade fluctuations, it is clear that a given real rate may not continue to be an equilibrium rate, as Diaz-Alejandro noted (1976, p. 15). It is an open question whether a small country, facing exogenous fluctuations in its terms of trade, should stabilize the real exchange rate at the mean terms of trade,[12] using fiscal and monetary policies to react to terms-of-trade changes, or whether, instead, the exchange rate is an optimal instrument.

---

[12] Note that once there are terms-of-trade fluctuations between traded goods, even the notion of a real exchange rate (defined as the relative price of tradables to home goods) is not well defined.

Even if the latter is correct, there is little guidance as to how the real exchange rate should behave.

As to the movement of a real equilibrium exchange rate over time, again there are no widely accepted answers. Bruno (1976) modeled a two-sector open economy with traded and nontraded goods. The country may borrow or lend but must end up with its initial level of indebtedness. In his model, the optimal path of the real exchange rate depends on whether or not the relative supply of tradables increases more than demand over time, as well as on other policy choices. Optimal borrowing, followed by later repayment, in the context of a constant relative supply of tradables, would imply gradual depreciation of the real exchange rate. To the extent that the relative supply of tradables was increasing, depreciation would be at a lower rate, and, if the increase was sufficiently great, the real exchange rate could even appreciate over time.

Thus, a priori there is little to suggest what the optimal time path of the real exchange rate might be. If one wishes to assert that there is no presumption that the relative supply of tradables will increase more than demand over time, then borrowing at earlier stages of development, followed by later repayment, would suggest a gradual depreciation of the real exchange rate. This, of course, presupposes that at the world real rate of interest, the available investment opportunities yielding at least that return exceed domestic savings during the early stages of development.

For policymakers concerned with liberalization and removal of exchange control, implicit PPP models are relied on, of which the crawling-peg model is one variety. Alternatively, of course, a country wishing to abandon its exchange-control regime could adopt a floating exchange rate, thereby avoiding the question of what the exchange rate should be. That raises the difficulties to be discussed next.

8.3.2 *Crawling pegs*

It will be recalled from Chapters 4 and 5 that most analyses of exchange-rate determination view the capital account as being the primary determinant of the exchange rate in the short run, with the current account responding to exchange-rate changes only slowly, and perhaps even perversely initially.

Black (1976) modeled the foreign-exchange market for a developing country where private capital flows do not exist and where only current-account transactions influence the foreign-exchange market. For the very short run, when the J curve may be operative (or when a country has sufficient monopoly power in trade), the private market may well be unstable. The proposition is a logical corollary to the notion that the capital account is what stabilizes the foreign-exchange market in the short run: If there is no private-capital market, the Central Bank must intervene for short-run stability.

This argument, which has been advanced by Branson and Katseli (1981*b*), among others, leads logically to the question what the pegging rule should be. This has a logical connection to the optimal intervention rules discussed in Section 6.3, but it also raises other issues.

There are two aspects to the pegging question. On one hand, there is the question what currency or currencies should be involved in the peg. On the other hand, there is the question of the rules by which the peg should be altered over time.

With regard to the choice of basket, the question is germane only in the case in which countries do not have highly concentrated trade with one currency area. If trade is concentrated, pegging to the currency is optimal. When trade is more diversified, the problem of choosing weights for currencies in the basket arises. Black (1976) proposed weights that would minimize the effects of changes in third-country exchange rates on the domestic price of traded goods or its ratio to the price of non-traded goods. Such a scheme entails weighting each currency in a basket of currencies by an amount determined according to the country's share of exports and imports, each in turn weighted by the country's monopoly power in export and import markets and by the share of exportables and import-competing goods in tradable production. For a small country with no monopoly power in trade, the weight for the ith country would be the (total, not country-specific) share of exportable production in tradable production times the ith country's share of the small country's imports.

Branson and Katseli (1981b) extended the analysis to cover cases in which the objective is to minimize fluctuations in the terms of trade induced by third-country currency fluctuations or to minimize the influence of third-country exchange-rate changes on the current-account balance. When terms of trade constitute the criterion, the question is relevant only when countries have asymmetric market power, as, for example, in exports and not in imports. Interestingly, under the Branson-Katseli objectives, the larger the share of country j as a buyer of i's exports, the smaller should be its weight in the basket if there is monopoly power in exporting.[13] Weighting schemes, of course, cover only the question of how the exchange rate should be determined at a given time. As pointed out by Branson and Katseli (1981b),

> weighting schemes . . . only eliminate the effects of fluctuations in third-currency exchange rates . . . on the relevant target variables for the home country. Simply pegging the price of the numeraire to any of these currency baskets will clearly not maintain external balance in almost all cases [Branson and Katseli, 1981b, p. 391].

They first proposed a gliding-peg rule (1981b) in which adjustment of the rate would be made in accordance with changes in the current-account balance. Later (1981a), they reworked their results to define a currency peg in terms of a "real exchange rate," so that the index of the real effective exchange rate became the weighted-average rate of increase in the nom-

---

[13] Mathieson (1976) showed that a crawling peg chosen to maximize welfare (e.g., sustainable real per-capita income) will generally lead to a different exchange-rate path than will a rule based on a stabilization target such as reserves or current-account balance.

inal exchange rate plus the foreign country's rate of price increase less the home country's rate of price increase. With this redefinition, they found that the results obtained earlier held for real-exchange-rate definitions.[14] Their formulas can thus be interpreted as justification of a crawling peg, where the crawl pertains to the differential in rates of inflation and the peg pertains to a basket of currencies. Branson and Katseli noted that maintenance of a crawling peg, regardless of the target, would not necessarily ensure external balance and that adjustments in the real rate might have to occur in response to imbalances.[15]

It will be recalled from Section 6.3 that Kenen (1975) investigated the properties of alternative rules for changing the (real) exchange rate, including a "gliding" peg, where adjustment would be undertaken according to various rules. Kenen's results were based on a simulation effort. More recently, Branson and de Macedo (1980) derived the Kenen results within an optimal-control framework, finding that a current-account (or flow) indicator is stable, but may generate large swings in reserves, whereas a reserve indicator for exchange-rate changes will yield a limit cycle. The optimal adjustment rule is a weighted combination of flow and stock targets, with an additional parameter reflecting the desired speed of adjustment. The precise weights, however, are very sensitive to the actual parameters.

8.4 Opening up

As already mentioned, the presence of binding quotas on imports and other exchange-control restrictions makes the process of devaluation different in exchange-control regimes

---

[14] They also concluded that the currency of trade (not the currency denomination of the payment) is appropriate for weighting, and they considered the problem of disaggregation among commodities. See also Branson and Katseli (1981*b*) for an analysis of the contribution of floating rates to terms-of-trade fluctuations among developing countries.

[15] There is a large literature on the macroeconomic response to the crawling peg that is not covered here. See Blejer and Leiderman (1981) and the references cited therein.

than it is when there is a change in parity of a convertible-currency country. Even when devaluation in an exchange-control context is intended simply to offset existing or anticipated differences in inflationary pressures, the fact that the change is discrete implies that there will be a short-run change in the domestic price of importables relative to exportables.

Many devaluations from a position of exchange control have been designed not to eliminate the exchange-control apparatus but rather to accompany efforts to reduce inflation or excess demand. These devaluation-antiinflationary packages have been termed "stabilization programs" by the IMF, and the intent is quite clearly to achieve "an improvement in the balance between supply and demand in an economy, aimed at moderating inflationary pressures and strengthening the balance of payments" (Crockett, 1981, p. 54). Hence, the targeting of these programs has been chiefly toward the restoration of macroeconomic balance.[16]

In addition to simple restoration of controls to the status quo ante, in which case the changing of the exchange rate resembles what would take place under a convertible currency with an above-average rate of inflation, two types of efforts to alter the regime have been analyzed. On one side, a number of efforts have been made to analyze the move toward a less "financially repressed" economy, to use McKinnon's apt phrase. On the other side, efforts have begun to analyze the interrelationships between opening up on current account and on capital account.

The former, which relates only indirectly to the role of the exchange rate in the economy, needs only brief mention. With slightly different approaches, Kapur (1976) and Mathieson (1980) have both argued for raising the nominal rate of interest, rather than lowering the rate of growth of the money supply, as the optimal monetary policy to accompany a devaluation when the initial situation is one of "financial repression" (with credit

---

[16] See Black (1981) and Krueger (1981) for discussions of stabilization programs. Crockett (1981) provided a summary of the issues as seen from the IMF's perspective.

rationing and poorly functioning domestic financial markets). Mathieson (1980), in particular, focused on the optimal time path of adjustment from negative real rates of interest with rapid monetary growth to a slower rate of monetary growth and positive real rates of interest. Concern centered on the financial difficulties that may be faced by important sectors of the economy in the short run. Mathieson found that gradual adjustments, and especially only a gradual lowering of the monetary growth rate, would lead to a smoother adjustment path. Not surprisingly, these results are sensitive to the specification of expectations within the model. Under rational expectations, the degree to which the interest rate rises initially is smaller, and the rate at which monetary growth is decelerated is greater, than under adaptive-expectations models.

Analysis of the interrelationships between current account and capital account (and the impact of a high degree of international capital mobility on the process of opening up) is more recent. In part, this is because in the 1960s countries attempting to change their exchange-control structure did so in the context of very limited capital mobility, if not one of complete restrictions.[17]

As pointed out in Section 8.1, it was earlier recognized that the initial impact of devaluation itself might be deflationary, in contrast to the conventional belief that it would necessarily be inflationary. Some authors, including Behrman (1976, Chapter 9) and Krueger (1978, Chapter 8 and Appendix), further

---

[17] South Korea induced sizable capital inflows in the late 1960s in the context of dollar-denominated foreign loans being available to domestic businessmen at rates of interest well below the domestic rate. This was because the rate of inflation in South Korea was above the world rate. The result was an opportunity to profit if debt could be repaid prior to devaluations. See Frank, Kim, and Westphal (1975, Chapter 7) for a description and analysis. The capital inflow experienced by South Korea was closely regulated by the government and was little noted at the time. By the late 1970s, large movements of funds characterized several opening-up efforts, especially in the Southern Cone, as noted by Diaz-Alejandro (1980).

pointed to the fact that devaluations from positions of extreme restrictions on imports were often accompanied by sizable official foreign loans (or even reversals of speculative capital flows), which in turn permitted sharp increases in imports, and even increased current-account deficits, following devaluations. These increased imports naturally exerted both deflationary pressure on the economy and downward pressure on the domestic relative price of import-competing goods. The latter could, in a sticky wage-price context, account for the frequently observed recessions that have accompanied devaluations.

The question of the optimal mix of exchange-rate changes and increased import inflows as a means of eliminating, or at least reducing, the differential between domestic and world relative prices of exportables and import-competing goods has not yet been resolved. Two issues are involved: First, there is the question whether once-and-for-all changes outperform gradual adjustments. Second, there are questions about the interactions between current account and capital account and the optimal timing of opening up these two separate components.[18]

Regarding the first issue, there is no systematic modeling of the problem, and the question whether or not policy changes should be gradual remains entirely open. It is evident, however, that different specifications of speeds of adjustment and of expectations will lead to a variety of different answers: Whenever expectations fully anticipate the outcome, gradualism can have appeal only if there are sticky prices or lagged adjustments somewhere within the system.

The second issue has already prompted some work. Dornbusch (1980c) modeled an initial inflationary situation in the context of a model with a home good and a single traded good. Home-goods output is demand-determined, as a function of the relative price of importables in terms of home goods, the real

---

[18] Related to this question is the interesting empirical problem of how the price levels in the Southern Cone countries (and especially Argentina) exceeded the prefixed rate of devaluation plus the world rate of inflation. See Calvo (1981) for a discussion.

rate of interest, and real income. Equilibrium in the money market is a function of real balances and real income, which determine the nominal interest rate. The current account of the balance of payments is a function of real income and the real exchange rate, whereas the capital-account balance is a function of the international interest-rate differential adjusted for differences in anticipated rates of inflation (under perfect foresight).

Under these assumptions, a reduction in the rate of inflation typically involves, in the short run, a real appreciation of the exchange rate, which implies (1) a higher price of nontraded goods, (2) a reduction in demand for home goods that is reflected in the short run in reduced real output, (3) an increased real interest rate, and (4) a payments surplus. Essentially, anticipations of a lower rate of inflation will shift demand toward holding higher money balances, which are compatible with equilibrium only with a lower real rate of interest. That, in turn, induces a capital inflow, which causes the real-exchange-rate appreciation. This appreciation is reversed in the long run as the steady state is attained, with the new, lower rate of inflation.

Dornbusch then assumed that the authorities follow a rule that sets the rate of change of the exchange rate equal to that of the domestic price level and also sets a fixed rate of growth of the money supply under adaptive expectations of the rate of inflation (based on observed money growth). Inflation thus responds sluggishly to observed money growth. If the authorities lower the rate of growth of the money supply, then

> when money growth is first reduced, there is no impact effect at all. Real balances start declining, as money growth now falls short of trend inflation expectation and thus of actual inflation. Only as real balances actually have declined, do we start having an effect. The real interest rate is rising and hence output starts falling. Together with the fall in output, which

> improves the current account, the rise in real interest
> rates improves the capital account. There is accord-
> ingly a balance of payments improvement or net
> reserve inflows. Inflation is decelerating [Dornbusch,
> 1980c, p. 139].

In Dornbusch's analysis, the real exchange rate appreciates
during the transition process both because of reduced real
income (recession) and because of capital inflows associated
with the higher real interest rate. His results stem primarily
from the assumption that inflation, for whatever reason, has a
life of its own and responds only with a lag to a changed rate of
monetary growth.

Calvo (1980) also analyzed the inflation-stabilization, capi-
tal-inflow nexus. In his model, the basic ingredient is that when
expectations of a lower rate of inflation are formed, maximizing
individuals shift their portfolios toward domestic assets (either
land or currency). Starting from a long-run equilibrium, lowering the rate of devaluation may lead to an instantaneous
appreciation of the real exchange rate above its long-term level
as individuals shift their portfolios toward domestic assets. This
capital inflow (or reversal of a capital outflow) leads to an
upward jump in the price level and a negative current-account
balance in the short run. Thereafter, the rate of increase of
domestic prices falls below its long-term rate (set by the rate of
monetary expansion and implicitly equal to the rate of devaluation plus the rate of world inflation). The initial jump in the
domestic price level (and appreciation of the real exchange rate
resulting therefrom) could, of course, be mistaken for accelerating inflation associated with a reduced rate of devaluation.

If, with the changed rate of devaluation, private holdings of
foreign assets are frozen at their initial levels (capital immobility), the real exchange rate will unambiguously depreciate, and
the possibility of a once-and-for-all appreciation of the
exchange rate and a jump in the price level no longer exists.
This result, if robust to other specifications of underlying mac-

roeconomic conditions and expectations, might be interpreted to mean that opening up should occur first on current account, and only later on capital account.

As this brief description indicates, the literature to date raises more questions than it answers regarding links between current account and capital account in opening up. It seems apparent that as additional research along these lines is undertaken, this is one of the areas in which our understanding will increase markedly.

REFERENCES

Aizenman, Joshua. 1981. "Devaluation and Liberalization in the Presence of Tariff and Quota Restrictions – An Equilibrium Model." *Journal of International Economics* 11(2):197–206.

Alexander, Sidney S. 1952. "Effects of a Devaluation on a Trade Balance." *IMF Staff Papers* 2:263–78 (reprinted by Caves and Johnson, 1968).

Aliber, Robert Z. 1973. "The Interest Rate Parity Theorem: A Reinterpretation." *Journal of Political Economy* 81(6):1451–9.

Allen, Polly R. 1973. "A Portfolio Approach to International Capital Flows." *Journal of International Economics* 3(2):135–60.

Allen Polly R., and Peter B. Kenen. 1980. *Asset Markets, Exchange Rates, and Economic Integration.* Cambridge University Press.

1976. "Portfolio Adjustment in Open Economies: A Comparison of Alternative Specifications." *Weltwirtschaftliches Archiv* 112(1):34–71.

Argy, Victor, and Michael Porter. 1972. "The Forward Exchange Market and the Effects of Domestic and External Disturbances under Alternative Exchange Rate Systems." *IMF Staff Papers* 19(3):503–32.

Armington, Paul S. 1969. "A Theory of Demand for Products Distinguished by Place of Production." *IMF Staff Papers* 16(2):179–201.

Aukrust, Odd. 1977. "Inflation in the Open Economy: A Norwegian Model." In Lawrence B. Krause and Walter S. Salant (eds.), *Worldwide Inflation: Theory and Recent Experience,* pp. 107–53. Washington, D.C.: Brookings Institution.

Bacha, Edmar, and Lance Taylor. 1971. "Foreign Exchange Shadow Prices: A Critical Review of Current Theories." *Quarterly Journal of Economics* 85(2):197–224.

Balassa, Bela. 1964. "The Purchasing-Power-Parity Doctrine: A Reappraisal." *Journal of Political Economy* 72:584–96.

Barro, Robert J. 1978. "A Stochastic Equilibrium Model of an Open Economy under Flexible Exchange Rates." *Quarterly Journal of Economics* 92:149–64.

Behrman, Jere R. 1976. *Foreign Trade Regimes and Economic Development: Chile.* New York: Columbia University Press for the National Bureau of Economic Research.

Berglas, Eytan, and Assaf Razin. 1973. "Real Exchange Rates and Devaluation." *Journal of International Economics* 3:179–92.

Bhagwati, Jagdish N. 1978. *Foreign Trade Regimes and Economic Development: Anatomy and Consequences of Exchange Control Regimes.* Cambridge, Mass.: Ballinger for the National Bureau of Economic Research.

Bigman, David, and Teizo Taya. 1980. *The Functioning of Floating Exchange Rates.* Cambridge, Mass.: Ballinger.

Bilson, John F. O. 1980. "The 'Speculative Efficiency' Hypothesis," NBER working paper no. 474.

——— 1979. "Recent Developments in Monetary Models of Exchange Rate Determination." *IMF Staff Papers* 26(2):201–23.

Black, Stanley W. 1981. "The Impact of Changes in the World Economy on Stabilization Policies in the 1970s." In William R. Cline and Sidney Weintraub (eds.), *Economic Stabilization in Developing Countries,* pp. 43–81. Washington, D.C.: Brookings Institution.

——— 1976. "Exchange Policies for Less Developed Countries in a World of Floating Rates." Essays in International Finance, no. 119. Princeton University.

——— 1973. *International Money Markets and Flexible Exchange Rates.* Princeton Studies in International Finance, no. 32. Princeton University Press.

Blejer, Mario I. 1978. "Exchange Restrictions and the Monetary Approach to the Exchange Rate." In Jacob Frenkel and Harry Johnson (eds.), *Economics of Exchange Rates: Selected Studies,* pp. 117–128. Reading, Mass.: Addison-Wesley.

Blejer, Mario I., and Leonardo Leiderman. 1981. "A Monetary Approach to the Crawling-Peg System: Theory and Evidence." *Journal of Political Economy* 89(1):132–51.

Blitzer, C., P. Dasgupta, and J. Stiglitz. 1981. "Project Appraisal and Foreign Exchange Constraints." *Economic Journal* 91(361):58–74.

Boyer, R. S. 1977. "Devaluation and Portfolio Balance." *American Economic Review* 67(2):54–63.

Boyer, Russell S. 1978. "Optimal Foreign Exchange Market Intervention." *Journal of Political Economy* 86(6):1045–55.

Branson, W. 1977. "Asset Markets and Relative Prices in Exchange Rate Determination." *Sozialwissenschaftliche Annalen* 1:69–89.

——— 1975. "Stocks and Flows in International Monetary Analysis." In A. Ando et al. (eds.), *International Aspects of Stabilization Policies,* pp. 27–50. Federal Reserve Bank of Boston.

——— 1972. "The Trade Effects of the 1971 Currency Realignments." *Brookings Papers on Economic Activity* 1:15–69.

Branson, William H., and Jorge Braga de Macedo. 1980. "The Optimal Weighting of Indicators for a Crawling Peg." NBER working paper no. 527.

Branson, W., H. Halttunen, and P. Masson. 1977. "Exchange Rates in the Short Run." *European Economic Review* 10:303–24.

Branson, William H., and Louka T. Katseli. 1981*a*. "Currency Baskets and Real Effective Exchange Rates." NBER working paper no. 666.

1981*b*. "Exchange Rate Policy in Developing Countries." In S. Grassman and E. Lundberg (eds.), *The World Economic Order: Past and Prospects*, pp. 391–419. London: Macmillan.

Branson, W., and Julio J. Rotemberg. 1980. "International Adjustment with Wage Rigidity." *European Economic Review* 13:309–32.

Bruno, Michael. 1979. "Stabilization and Stagflation in a Semi-Industrialized Economy." In Rudiger Dornbusch and Jacob Frenkel (eds.), *International Economic Policy: Theory and Evidence*, pp. 270–89. Baltimore: Johns Hopkins University Press.

1978. "Exchange Rates, Import Costs, and Wage-Price-Dynamics." *Journal of Political Economy* 86:379–403.

1976. "The Two-Sector Open Economy and the Real Exchange Rate." *American Economic Review* 66:566–77.

Bruno, Michael, and Hollis Chenery. 1962. "Development Alternatives in an Open Economy: The Case of Israel." *Economic Journal* 72:79–103.

Bruno, Michael, and Jeffrey Sachs. 1979. "Macro-economic Adjustment with Import Price Shocks: Real and Monetary Aspects." NBER working paper no. 340.

Buiter, Willem H., and Douglas D. Purvis. 1980. "Oil, Disinflation, and Export Competitiveness: A Model of the 'Dutch Disease'." NBER working paper no. 592.

Calvo, Guillermo. 1981. "Trying to Stabilize: Some Theoretical Reflections Based on the Case of Argentina." Mimeograph.

1980. "Financial Opening, Crawling Peg and the Real Exchange Rate." Mimeograph.

Calvo, G., and C. Rodriguez. 1977. "A Model of Exchange Rate Determination under Currency Substitution and Rational Expectations." *Journal of Political Economy* 85:617–25.

Casas, F. R. 1975. "Efficient Macroeconomic Stabilization Policies under Floating Exchange Rates." *International Economic Review* 16(3):682–98.

Caves, E., and H. G. Johnson (eds.). 1968. *A.E.A. Readings in International Economics, Vol. XI.* Homewood, Ill.: Irwin.

Chenery, Hollis B., and Alan M. Strout. 1966. "Foreign Assistance and Economic Development." *American Economic Review* 56:679–733.

Clower, Robert W. 1967. "A Reconsideration of the Micro-foundations of Monetary Theory." *Western Economic Journal* 6(1):1–8.

Cooper, Richard N. 1971. "Devaluation and Aggregate Demand in Aid-Receiving Countries." In J. Bhagwati, R. Jones, R. Mundell, and J. Vanek (eds.), *Trade, Balance of Payments and Growth*, pp. 355–76. Amsterdam: North Holland.

Corden, W. M. 1977. *Inflation, Exchange Rates, and the World Economy.* University of Chicago Press.

1960. "The Geometric Representation of Policies to Attain Internal and External Balance." *Review of Economic Studies* 28:1–22.

Corden, W. M., and J. Peter Neary. 1980. "Booming Sector and Deindustrialization in a Small Open Economy." Mimeograph.

Crockett, Andrew D. 1981. "Stabilization Policies in Developing Countries: Some Policy Considerations." *IMF Staff Papers* 28(1):54–79.

Cuddington, John T. 1981. "Import Substitution Policies: A Two-Sector, Fix-Price Model." *Review of Economic Studies* 48:327–42.

1980. "Fiscal and Exchange Rate Policies in a Fix-Price Trade Model with Export Rationing." *Journal of International Economics* 10:319–40.

Darby, Michael R. 1980. "Does Purchasing Power Parity Work?" NBER working paper no. 607.

de Macedo, Jorge Braga. 1980. "Exchange Rate Behavior with Currency Inconvertibility." Mimeograph. Princeton University.

Dervis, Kemal. 1980. "Analyzing the Resource Pull Effects of Devaluation under Exchange Control." *Journal of Development Economics* 7(1):23–47.

Diaz-Alejandro, Carlos. 1980. "Southern Cone Stabilization Plans." Mimeograph. Fundacao Getulio Vargas, Rio de Janeiro.

1976. *Foreign Trade Regimes and Economic Development: Colombia.* New York: Columbia University Press.

1963. "A Note on the Impact of Devaluation and the Redistributive Effect." *Journal of Political Economy* 71:577–80.

Dixit, A. 1978. "The Balance of Trade in a Model of Temporary Equilibrium with Rationing." *Review of Economic Studies* 65(3):393–404.

Dooley, Michael P., and Peter Isard. 1980. "Capital Controls, Political Risk, and Deviations from Interest-Rate Parity." *Journal of Political Economy* 88(2):370–84.

Dornbusch, Rudiger. 1980*a*. "Exchange Rate Economics: Where Do We Stand?" *Brookings Papers on Economic Activity* 1:143–85.

1980*b*. "Monetary Policy under Exchange Rate Flexibility." In David Bigman and Teizo Taya (eds.), *The Functioning of Floating Exchange Rates: Theory, Evidence and Policy Implications,* pp. 3–31. Cambridge, Mass.: Ballinger.

1980*c*. "Inflation Stabilization and Capital Mobility." NBER working paper no. 555.

1976. "Expectations and Exchange Rate Dynamics." *Journal of Political Economy* 84:1161–76.

1975*a*. "A Portfolio Balance Model of the Open Economy." *Journal of Monetary Economics* 1:3–20.

1975*b*. "Exchange Rates and Fiscal Policy in a Popular Model of International Trade." *American Economic Review* 65:859–71.

1973*a*. "Currency Depreciation, Hoarding, and Relative Prices." *Journal of Political Economy* 81(4):893–915.

1973*b*. "Devaluation, Money and Non-Traded Goods." *American Economic Review* 63:871–80.

Dornbusch, R., and S. Fischer. 1980. "Exchange Rates and the Current Account." *American Economic Review* 70:960–71.

Fama, Eugene F., and Andre Farber. 1979. "Money, Bonds and Foreign Exchange." *American Economic Review* 69:639–49.

Findlay, Ronald. 1980. "Oil Supplies and Employment Levels: A Simple Macro Model." In John S. Chipman and Charles P. Kindleberger (eds.), *Flexible Exchange Rates and the Balance of Payments.* Amsterdam: North Holland.

Findlay, Ronald, and Carlos Rodriguez. 1977. "Intermediate Imports and Macroeconomic Policy under Flexible Exchange Rates." *Canadian Journal of Economics* 10:208–17.

Fischer, Stanley. 1977. "Stability and Exchange Rate Systems in a Monetarist Model of the Balance of Payments." In Robert Z. Aliber (ed.), *The Political Economy of Monetary Reform,* pp. 59–73. New York: Macmillan.

Fishelson, Gideon. 1976. "The Exchange Rate in a Controlled Foreign Exchange Market (Israel)." Working paper no. 32-76. Foerder Institute for Economic Research, Tel Aviv University.

Flanders, M. June, and Elhanan Helpman. 1978. "On Exchange Rate Policies for a Small Country." *Economic Journal* 88(349):44–58.

Fleming, J. Marcus. 1971. "Dual Exchange Rates for Current and Capital Transactions: A Theoretical Examination." In *Essays in International Economics.* Cambridge: Harvard University Press.

1962. "Domestic Financial Policies under Fixed and Floating Exchange Rates." *IMF Staff Papers* 9:369–79.

Frank, Charles R., Kwang Suk Kim, and Larry E. Westphal. 1975. *Foreign Trade Regimes and Economic Development: South Korea.* New York: Columbia University Press for the National Bureau of Economic Research.

Frenkel, Jacob A. 1980*a.* "The Collapse of Purchasing Power Parities during the 1970s." NBER working paper no. 569. *European Economic Review* 16:145–65.

1980*b.* "The Demand for International Reserves under Pegged and Flexible Exchange Rate Regimes and Aspects of the Economics of Managed Float." In David Bigman and Teizo Taya (eds.), *The Functioning of Floating Exchange Rates: Theory, Evidence, and Policy Implications,* pp. 169–95. Cambridge, Mass.: Ballinger.

1976. "A Monetary Approach to the Exchange Rate: Doctrinal Aspects and Empirical Evidence." *Scandinavian Journal of Economics* 2:200–24.

Frenkel, Jacob A., and Harry G. Johnson. 1978. *The Economics of Exchange Rates: Selected Studies.* Reading, Mass.: Addison-Wesley.

1976. *The Monetary Approach to the Balance of Payments.* London: Allen & Unwin.

Frenkel, Jacob A., and Carlos A. Rodriguez. 1981. "Exchange Rate Dynamics and the Overshooting Hypothesis." Mimeograph. Presented at Segunda Conferencia Internacional sobre el Desarollo Financiero de America Latina y el Caribe, Caracas, April 2–4, 1981.

1975. "Portfolio Equilibrium and the Balance of Payments: A Monetary Approach." *American Economic Review* 65:674–88.

Friedman, Milton. 1953. "The Case for Flexible Exchange Rates." In Friedman, *Essays in Positive Economics*. University of Chicago Press (reprinted in abridged form by Caves and Johnson, 1968).

Girton, Lance, and Don Roper. 1976. "Theory and Implications of Currency Substitution." Unpublished. University of Utah.

Goldstein, Morris. 1980. *Have Flexible Exchange Rates Handicapped Macroeconomic Policy?* International Finance Section, Princeton Special Papers in International Economics, No. 14.

Grassman, Sven. 1973. *Exchange Reserves and the Financial Structure of Foreign Trade*. Lexington, Mass.: Lexington Books.

Hahn, Frank. 1959. "The Balance of Payments in a Monetary Economy." *Review of Economic Studies* 26(70):149–58.

Harberger, Arnold C. 1950. "Currency Depreciation, Income, and the Balance of Trade." *Journal of Political Economy* 58:47–60.

Hause, John C. 1966. "The Welfare Costs of Disequilibrium Exchange Rates." *Journal of Political Economy* 74:333–52.

Helpman, E. 1977. "Nontraded Goods and Macroeconomic Policy Under a Fixed Exchange Rate." *Quarterly Journal of Economics* 91:469–80.

1976. "Macroeconomic Policy in a Model of International Trade with a Wage Restriction." *International Economic Review* 17:262–77.

Helpman, Elhanan, and Assaf Razin. 1981. "Comparative Dynamics of Monetary Policy in a Floating Exchange Rate Regime." Foerder Institute for Economic Research, working paper no. 9-81.

1980. "A Comparison of Exchange Rate Regimes in the Presence of Imperfect Capital Markets." Seminar paper ISSN 0347-8769m, Institute for International Economic Studies, Stockholm.

1979. "Towards a Consistent Comparison of Alternative Exchange Rate Regimes." *Canadian Journal of Economics* 12(3):394–409.

Isard, P. 1977. "How Far Can We Push the Law of One Price?" *American Economic Review* 67:942–8.

Johnson, Harry G. 1977. "The Monetary Approach to the Balance of Payments: A Non-Technical Guide." *Journal of International Economics* 7:251–68.

1970. "The Case for Flexible Exchange Rates, 1969." *Federal Reserve Bank of St. Louis Review* 52:12–24.

1958. "Towards a General Theory of the Balance of Payments." In H. G. Johnson (ed.), *International Trade and Economic Growth*, pp. 153–68. London: Allen & Unwin.

Jones R. W. 1974. "Trade with Nontraded Goods: The Anatomy of Interconnected Markets." *Economica* 41:121–38.

1971. "The Three-Factor Model in Theory, Trade, and History," In J. Bhagwati et al. (eds.), *Trade, Balance of Payments, and Growth*, pp. 3–21. Amsterdam: North Holland.

1970. "The Transfer Problem Reconsidered." *Economica* 37:178–84.

1961. "Stability Conditions in International Trade: A General Equilibrium Analysis," *International Economic Review* 2:199–299.

Jones, R. W., and W. M. Corden. 1976. "Devaluation, Non-Flexible Prices, and the Trade Balance for a Small Country," *Canadian Journal of Economics* 9:150–61.

Kapur, Basant K. 1976. "Alternative Stabilization Policies for Less-Developed Economies," *Journal of Political Economy* 84:777–95.

Kareken, John, and Neil Wallace. 1977. "Portfolio Autarky: A Welfare Analysis," *Journal of International Economics* 7(1):19–44.

Katseli-Papaefstratiou, Louka T. 1979. *The Reemergence of the Purchasing Power Parity Doctrine in the 1970s.* International Finance Section, Special Papers in International Economics No. 13. Princeton University.

Kemp, Murray C. 1970. "The Balance of Payments and the Terms of Trade in Relation to Financial Controls." *Review of Economic Studies* 37(1):25–31.

    1962. "The Rate of Exchange, the Terms of Trade and the Balance of Payments in Fully Employed Economies." *International Economic Review* 3:314–27.

Kenen, Peter B. 1975. "Floats, Glides and Indicators: A Comparison of Methods for Changing Exchange Rates." *Journal of International Economics* 5(2):108–51.

Kindleberger, C. P. 1973. *The World in Depression 1929–1939.* London: Lane.

Kouri, Pentti J. K. 1978. "Balance of Payments and the Foreign Exchange Market: A Dynamic Partial Equilibrium Model." Cowles Foundation discussion paper no. 510.

    1976. "The Exchange Rate and the Balance of Payments in the Short Run and in the Long Run." *Scandinavian Journal of Economics* 78(1):255–75.

Kouri, Pentti J. K., and Michael G. Porter. 1974. "International Capital Flows and Portfolio Equilibrium." *Journal of Political Economy* 82:443–67.

Kravis, Irving B., and Z. Kennessey, A. Heston, and R. Summers. 1974. *A System of International Comparisons of Gross Product and Purchasing Power.* Baltimore: Johns Hopkins University Press.

Kravis, I. B., and R. E. Lipsey. 1978. "Price Behavior in the Light of Balance of Payments Theories." *Journal of International Economics* 8:193–246.

Krueger, Anne O. 1981. "Interactions between Inflation and Trade Regime Objectives in Stabilization Programs." In William R. Cline and Sidney Weintraub (eds.), *Economic Stabilization in Developing Countries,* pp. 83–114. Washington, D.C.: Brookings Institution.

    1978. *Foreign Trade Regimes and Economic Development: Liberalization Attempts and Consequences.* Cambridge, Mass.: Ballinger for the National Bureau of Economic Research.

    1974. "The Role of Home Goods and Money in Exchange Rate Adjustment." In Willy Sellekaerts (ed.), *International Trade and Finance,* pp. 141–61. London: Macmillan.

    1965. "The Impact of Alternative Government Policies under Varying Exchange Rate Systems." *Quarterly Journal of Economics* 79:195–206.

Krugman, Paul R., and Lance Taylor. 1978. "Contractionary Effects of Devaluation." *Journal of International Economics* 8(3):445–56.

Lapan, H. E., and W. Enders. 1980. "Random Disturbances and the Choice of Exchange Regimes in an Intergenerational Model." *Journal of International Economics* 10:263–83.

Laursen, Svend, and Lloyd A. Metzler. 1950. "Flexible Exchange Rates and the Theory of Employment." *Review of Economics and Statistics* 32:281–99.

Levich, Richard M. 1979a. "Analyzing the Accuracy of Foreign Exchange Advisory Services: Theory and Evidence." NBER working paper no. 336.

———. 1979b. "On the Efficiency of Markets for Foreign Exchange." In R. Dornbusch and J. Frenkel (eds.), *International Economic Policy: An Assessment of the Theory and Evidence,* pp. 246–67. Baltimore: Johns Hopkins University Press.

Liviatan, Nissan. 1979. "A Disequilibrium Analysis of the Monetary Trade Model." *Journal of International Economics* 9(3):355–77.

Lucas, R. E. 1972. "Expectations and the Neutrality of Money." *Journal of Economic Theory* 4(2):103–24.

McKinnon, Ronald I. 1981. "The Exchange Rate and Macroeconomic Policy: Changing Postwar Perceptions." Stanford University Center for Research in Economic Growth.

———. 1979. *Money in International Exchange.* Oxford University Press.

———. 1973. *Money and Capital in Economic Development.* Washington, D.C.: Brookings Institution.

———. 1969. "Portfolio Balance and International Payments Adjustment." In Robert A. Mundell and Alexander K. Swoboda (eds.), *Monetary Problems of the International Economy,* pp. 199–234. University of Chicago Press.

McKinnon, Ronald, and Wallace Oates. 1966. *The Implications of International Economic Integration for Monetary, Fiscal, and Exchange-Rate Policy.* Princeton Studies in International Finance No. 16.

Magee, Stephen P. 1973. "Currency Contracts, Pass Through and Devaluation." *Brookings Papers on Economic Activity* 1:303–25.

Mathieson, Donald J. 1980. "Financial Reform and Stabilization Policy in a Developing Economy." *Journal of Development Economics* 7:359–95.

———. 1976. "Is There an Optimal Crawl?" *Journal of International Economics* 6(2):183–202.

Meade, James E. 1956. "The Price Adjustment and the Australian Balance of Payments." *Economic Record* 32:239–56.

———. 1951. *The Balance of Payments.* Oxford University Press.

Michaely, Michael. 1960. "Relative-Prices and Income-Absorption Approaches to Devaluation: A Partial Reconciliation." *American Economic Review* 50:144–7.

Miles, Marc A. 1978. "Currency Substitution, Flexible Exchange Rates, and Monetary Independence." *American Economic Review* 68:428–36.

Modigliani, Franco, and Tommaso Padoa-Schioppa. 1978. *The Management of an Open Economy with '100% plus' Wage Indexation.* Essays in International Finance No. 130. Princeton University, International Finance Section.

Mundell, Robert. 1963. "Capital Mobility and Stabilization Policy under Fixed and Flexible Exchange Rates." *Canadian Journal of Economics and Political Science* 29:475–85.

    1960. "The Monetary Dynamics of International Adjustment under Fixed and Flexible Exchange Rates." *Quarterly Journal of Economics* 74:227–57.

Mussa, Michael. 1979. "Macroeconomic Interdependence and the Exchange Rate Regime." In Rudiger Dornbusch and Jacob A. Frenkel (eds.), *International Economic Policy: Theory and Evidence,* pp. 160–99. Baltimore: Johns Hopkins University Press.

    1976. "The Exchange Rate, the Balance of Payments and Monetary and Fiscal Policy under a Regime of Controlled Floating." *Scandinavian Journal of Economics* 2:229–48.

Neary, J. Peter. 1980. "Nontraded Goods and the Balance of Trade in a Neo-Keynesian Temporary Equilibrium." *Quarterly Journal of Economics* 95(3):403–29.

Negishi, Takashi. 1968. "Approaches to the Analysis of Devaluation." *International Economic Review* 9:218–27.

Niehans, Jürg. 1977. "Exchange Rate Dynamics with Stock/Flow Interaction." *Journal of Political Economy* 85(6):1245–57.

Obstfeld, Maurice. 1980a. "Imperfect Asset Substitutability and Monetary Policy under Fixed Exchange Rates." *Journal of International Economics* 10(2):177–200.

    1980b. "Intermediate Imports, the Terms of Trade, and the Dynamics of the Exchange Rate and Current Account." *Journal of International Economics* 10(4):461–80.

Officer, Lawrence. 1976. "The Purchasing-Power Parity Theory of Exchange Rates: A Review Article." *IMF Staff Papers* 23(1):1–60.

    1974. "Purchasing Power Parity and Factor Price Equalization." *Kyklos* 27(4):868–78.

Oppenheimer, Peter M. 1974. "Non-Traded Goods and the Balance of Payments: A Historical Note." *Journal of Economic Literature* 12(3):882–8.

Pearce, I. F. 1961. "The Problem of the Balance of Payments." *International Economic Review* 2(1):1–28.

Polak, J. J. 1977. "Monetary Analysis of Income Formation and Payments Problems." *IMF Staff Papers* Vol. 6:1–50 (reprinted in *The Monetary Approach to the Balance of Payments.* Washington, D.C.: International Monetary Fund).

Prais, S. J. 1961. "Some Mathematical Notes on the Quantity Theory of Money in an Open Economy." *IMF Staff Papers* 8(1):212–21 (reprinted in *The Monetary Approach to the Balance of Payments.* Washington, D.C.: International Monetary Fund).

Razin, Assaf. 1981. "Exchange Rate Dynamics." Mimeograph. Tel Aviv University.

    1980. "Capital Movements, Intersectoral Resource Shifts, and the Trade Balance." Seminar paper no. 159. Institute for International Economic Studies, Stockholm.

Rodriguez, Carlos A. 1980. "The Role of Trade Flows in Exchange Rate Determination: A Rational Expectations Approach." *Journal of Political Economy* 88(6):1148–58.

    1979. "Short- and Long-Run Effects of Monetary and Fiscal Policies under Flexible Exchange Rates and Perfect Capital Mobility." *American Economic Review* 69(1):176–82.

Sachs, Jeffrey D. 1981. "The Current Account and Macroeconomic Adjustment in the 1970s." *Brookings Papers on Economic Activity* 1:201–68.

    1980. "Wages, Flexible Exchange Rates, and Macroeconomic Policy." *Quarterly Journal of Economics* 94:731–47.

    1979. "Wages, Profits, and Macroeconomic Adjustment: A Comparative Study." *Brookings Papers on Economic Activity* 2:269–319.

Salter, W. A. 1959. "Internal and External Balance: The Role of Price and Expenditure Effects." *Economic Record* 35:226–38.

Samuelson, Paul A. 1971. "On the Trail of Conventional Beliefs about the Transfer Problem." in Jagdish Bhagwati et al. (eds.), *Trade, Balance of Payments, and Growth,* pp. 327–51. New York: North Holland/American Elsevier.

    1966. "Theoretical Notes on Trade Problems." In Joseph E. Stiglitz (ed.), *The Collected Scientific Papers of Paul A. Samuelson, Vol. 2,* pp. 821–30. Cambridge: M.I.T. Press.

Sheikh, M. A. 1976. "Black Market for Foreign Exchange, Capital Flows, and Smuggling." *Journal of Development Economics* 3(1):9–26.

Sohmen, Egon. 1958. "The Effect of Devaluation on the Price Level." *Quarterly Journal of Economics* 72:273–83.

Southard, Frank A., Jr. 1979. *The Evolution of the International Monetary Fund.* Essays in International Finance No. 135. Princeton University, International Finance Section.

Stockman, Alan C. 1980. "A Theory of Exchange Rate Determination." *Journal of Political Economy* 88(4):673–98.

Svensson, Lars E. O., and Assaf Razin. 1981. "The Terms of Trade, Spending, and the Current Account: The Harberger-Laursen-Metzler Effect." Institute for International Economic Studies seminar paper no. 170.

Swan, Trevor. 1960. "Economic Control in a Dependent Economy." *Economic Record* 36:51–66.

Swoboda, Alexander. 1974. "The Dual Exchange Rate System and Monetary Independence." In Robert Z. Aliber (ed.), *National Monetary Policies and the International Financial System,* pp. 258–70. University of Chicago Press.

Tower, Edward, and Thomas D. Willett. 1976. *The Theory of Optimum Currency Areas and Exchange Rate Flexibility.* Special Papers in International Economics No. 11. Princeton University, International Finance Section.

Turnovsky, Stephen J. 1981. "The Effects of Devaluation and Foreign Price Disturbances under Rational Expectations." *Journal of International Economics* 11(1):33–60.

———. 1979a. "On the Insulation Properties of Flexible Exchange Rates." *Revue Economique* 30(4):719–46.

———. 1979b. "Monetary Policy and Foreign Price Disturbances under Flexible Exchange Rates: A Stochastic Approach." Discussion paper no. 79-125, University of Minnesota Center for Economic Research.

Van Duyne, Carl. 1980. "Imperfect Foresight and the Insulation Properties of a Flexible Exchange Rate." *Scandinavian Journal of Economics* 3:352–61.

van Wijnbergen, Sweder. 1980. "Oil Price Shocks and the Current Account: An Analysis of Short Run Adjustment Measures." Mimeograph. World Bank.

Wallace, Neil. 1979. "Why Markets in Foreign Exchange Are Different from Other Markets." *Federal Reserve Bank of Minneapolis, Quarterly Review* 3(4):1–7.

Whitman, Marina V. N. 1975. "Global Monetarism and the Monetary Approach to the Balance of Payments." *Brookings Papers on Economic Activity* 3:491–536.

Williamson, John. 1977. *The Failure of World Monetary Reform, 1971–74.* New York University Press.

Wilson, Charles A. 1979. "Anticipated Shocks and Exchange Rate Dynamics." *Journal of Political Economy* 87(3):639–47.

SUBJECT INDEX

207

AUTHOR INDEX

217